TRANSFORMING THE [
SOCIAL MOVEMENTS AND THE WORLD-SYSTEM

TRANSFORMING THE REVOLUTION
SOCIAL MOVEMENTS AND THE WORLD-SYSTEM

Samir Amin
Giovanni Arrighi
Andre Gunder Frank
Immanuel Wallerstein

AAKAR

Transforming the Revolution: Social Movements and the World-System
Samir Amin, Giovanni Arrighi, Andre Gunder Frank and
Immanuel Wallerstein

© Samir Amin, Giovanni Arrighi, Andre Gunder Frank and
Immanuel Wallerstein 1990
© Aakar Books for South Asia 2006

First Published in India 2006
Reprinted 2009
Reprinted 2018

ISBN 978-81-87879-95-4

Published in agreement with Monthly Review Press, New York

All rights reserved. No part of this book may be reproduced or transmitted, in any form or by any means, without the prior permission of the publisher.

Published by
AAKAR BOOKS
28 E Pocket IV, Mayur Vihar Phase I
Delhi 110 091, India
aakarbooks@gmail.com
www.aakarbooks.com

Printed at
Sapra Brothers, Delhi 110 092

CONTENTS

Prefatory Note	7
Introduction: Common Premises *Samir Amin, Giovanni Arrighi, Andre Gunder Frank, and Immanuel Wallerstein*	9
Antisystemic Movements: History and Dilemmas *Immanuel Wallerstein*	13
Marxist Century—American Century: The Making and Remaking of the World Labor Movement *Giovanni Arrighi*	54
The Social Movements in the Periphery: An End to National Liberation? *Samir Amin*	96
Civil Democracy: Social Movements in Recent World History *Andre Gunder Frank and Marta Fuentes*	139
Conclusion: A Friendly Debate *Samir Amin, Giovanni Arrighi, Andre Gunder Frank, and Immanuel Wallerstein*	181

PREFATORY NOTE

This book was completed in mid-1989. It is being published in the fall of 1990. In between, the dramatic events of eastern Europe have occurred. They are not mentioned in this book.

We are publishing it as we wrote it because we do not believe these events force us to change anything of significance in the book. Indeed it is precisely because such events are part of the larger ongoing pattern discussed in this book that we believe it is necessary to "transform the revolution."

—The Authors

INTRODUCTION: COMMON PREMISES

Samir Amin, Giovanni Arrighi,
Andre Gunder Frank, and Immanuel Wallerstein

In 1982 we published a book entitled *Dynamics of Global Crisis*. It has been translated into French, Spanish, Turkish, Serbo-Croat, and German. That book was a statement of our separate and joint views on the historical development of the capitalist world-economy and the long-term "crisis" into which, in our view, it had entered. The book was an exploration of our partially convergent but also somewhat divergent perspectives on the nature of that "crisis."

We emphasized in the Introduction to the previous book a set of common and linked premises which we believe mark off our mode of analysis from that of many others: the existence since the sixteenth century of something that may be called a capitalist world-economy; a holistic framework of analysis of this capitalist world-economy; a belief that, despite increasing opposition to the world-system, the world socialist movement is in trouble both in praxis and in theory; the reality of U.S. hegemony since 1945 and the fact that this hegemony had now passed its peak; and the *worldwide* character of the so-called crisis.

These remain our premises. We feel that the concrete developments since 1982 have confirmed what we argued then. At that time we argued against a faddish view that the OPEC oil price rise was the "cause" of the difficulties of the world-economy in the 1970s. Does anyone today even remember that viewpoint? Today, writing in 1989, we believe that the view that the return in the 1980s to classical economic liberalism throughout the world-economy (West, East, and South) as the solution to current economic difficulties is equally faddish. We believe that a decade from now this view will seem as quaint as the views on OPEC's role in the 1970s seem today.

Why then a second book? This book is not about the "crisis" in the capitalist world-economy. Rather it is about what some believe to be the "crisis" in the movements. The language of the authors about the "movements" differs somewhat, as the reader will see. We refer to them variously as antisystemic, or social, or popular. The key point is that we all believe that, for at least 150 years, if not longer, there have existed multiple movements throughout the world-system that have protested and organized against the multiple injustices of the existing system and have offered alternatives which they believed would bring about a fundamental change in and/or improvement of the situation. It is the history and the contemporary dilemmas of such movements that are the object of our analyses here.

We believe that we cannot begin to appreciate this history or these current dilemmas without placing these movements within the framework of the historical evolution of the capitalist world-economy as a whole, of which these movements themselves have been an integral part.

We have defined the movements that fall within our purview very broadly. They include what have been called socialist or labor movements, nationalist or national liberation movements, peasant movements, women's movements, peace and ecology movements, even some religious movements. We have included such movements within our purview whenever and wherever their basic demands have been for greater democracy and greater equality in the world, and whenever they have thought of themselves as working to achieve such ends. In that sense, we have taken the classical slogan of "liberty, equality, and fraternity" not as the aspirations of bourgeois liberalism but as the incarnation of socialist, democratic demands of the world's ordinary people (or working classes).

This therefore implies two things about the movements. Not every "movement" that has existed belongs in this camp. There are some movements that have always moved in the opposite direction. In addition, many movements have changed colors or shifted emphases in the course of their organizational evolution. Which movements these are, and why the changes occurred, is precisely one of the themes these essays discuss. Obviously, not everyone will agree on the evaluation of particular movements at particular moments of their history. We often disagree among ourselves. We should also make clear our position on the historic role of states such as the USSR and the People's Republic of China. We differ about the degree (even the very reality) of their historic delinking from the capitalist world-economy. Our divergences, which were laid out in the previous book, appear once again in the essays in this book. We all, however, share deep reservations about the achievements of "real existing socialism," without in any way renouncing our deep reservations about the achievements of "real existing capitalism."

In sum, we believe that antisystemic, social, popular movements have been important in the modern world, despite the recurrent ambiguities surrounding their role. We think it crucial, however, to utilize a broad definition of what might be included under the rubric of an antisystemic or social or popular movement, and to refuse the exclusions and anathemas that many of these movements have at times placed on others of these movements.

Finally, we have written this book today on the antisystemic, social, popular movements because we believe that today these movements represent the key lever, and even the key locus, of social transformation. We are convinced that these movements are today, in the light of their own history of successes and failures, transforming the revolutionary process itself. Hence our title.

None of us thinks that the process of social transformation to come will be facile, and none of us believes there is any guarantee that the outcome will inevitably be progressive. But all of us agree that the present world-system, with its current structure (current meaning for the past several centuries) cannot survive eternally. The system will be transformed. It is historically possible (but not certain) that the transformation will be for the good, that is, result in a new world-system that will be more democratic and more egalitarian. We all believe that, if we are to move in this direction, it will be primarily the doing of the movements. Consequently, the struggles within the movements themselves about strategy and tactics are of fundamental significance. We write this book in the hope that we can aid the process by helping to perceive the dilemmas more clearly.

We have assigned ourselves a division of labor in this book. The first essay, by Immanuel Wallerstein, presents an historic overview of all the movements. It seeks to place their multiple varieties in relation to each other, and offers an explanation of why the movements for greater democracy and equality have taken such diverse forms. The second essay, by Giovanni Arrighi, concentrates on those movements that have been historically based on the working class or proletariat, which first appeared in Western Europe and North America. The third essay, by Samir Amin, concentrates on the movements that have been historically constructed by peoples in the periphery of the world-system, which placed the goal of "national liberation" at or near the top of their agenda. The fourth essay, by Andre Gunder Frank and Marta Fuentes, treats the "other" movements, those whose objectives were defined neither as proletarian power nor as national liberation. This is a diverse group, and some might think merely a residual category. In contemporary analyses, these "other" movements are sometimes referred to as "new social movements," a categorization Frank and Fuentes, however, eschew.

There are two reasons for this division of labor among the four essays. On the one hand, it represents an effort to achieve coverage in some depth of a very complex story. But, in addition, the division of labor reflects differences in emphasis among us, as the reader will see. We shall discuss these differences in some detail in the concluding chapter.

ANTISYSTEMIC MOVEMENTS: HISTORY AND DILEMMAS

Immanuel Wallerstein

1. The Creation of Antisystemic Movements and the Debate About Strategy, 1789–1945

The capitalist world-economy has been in existence for at least 500 years. Its early years were marked by considerable labor unrest, which took many forms, from peasant rebellion to food riots to messianic movements to banditry. But it was not until sometime in the nineteenth century that continuing organized antisystemic political movements of the oppressed strata were first formed. In itself, this was a remarkable social *invention*, which has too long gone unheralded and unanalyzed.

This social invention, this mechanism of social change, was very efficacious, but it also had limitations, and it is this double reality which explains the curious phenomenon of the post-1945 period. Never did antisystemic movements seem stronger than in the period after 1945. But never did more people have doubts that these movements were achieving their aims. This seeming anomaly has been the result of contradictory pressures deriving from the very structure and strategies of these movements.

The post-1945 history of these movements can only be understood or appreciated in the context of their history as organized continuing movements. And this history must perforce start with the French Revolution. It is not that the French Revolution, followed by the Napoleonic era, created the organizational bases of these movements. It did not, although of course we can find in embryo the structures that would emerge at a later time. It is rather that the French Revolution did two things. It put the ideology of the *Ancien Régime* permanently on the defensive, and throughout the world-system. And it simultaneously firmly established the ideological motifs of the modern world, the rallying cries and the rationale of the movements to come. These motifs can be plainly summarized in the French Revolution's famous slogan, "liberty, equality, fraternity."

On the one hand, this slogan inspired what in its broadest sense came to be called the social movement—that is, the struggle of the oppressed "working classes" to obtain liberty (full rights of political participation, access to a secure economic base to make possible political and social choice, social control over the workplace and living space), equality (elimination of political, economic, and social differentials), and fraternity (mutual aid and solidarity of the working classes which would thereby make possible the fraternity of all humanity).

The ideals of the social movement were not invented at the time of the French Revolution. They have a long history, often nurtured by movements of religious revolt. The French Revolution affected these ideals in three ways. First, it firmly established a secular form for these ideals. Second, it made them socially legitimate, to the point that, in the aftermath of the French Revolution, we have for the first time self-consciously *conservative* thinkers (such as DeMaistre) who set themselves the task of combatting these ideals, thereby recognizing their social force. Third, it spread these ideals throughout the world (most immediately the European world), and thereby made them global ideals, rising above an association with particular localities, groups, peoples.

On the other hand, the ideals of the French Revolution also inspired what in its broadest sense came to be called the national movement—that is, the struggle of the oppressed "peoples" to obtain liberty (their political, economic, and cultural autonomy as a collective group), equality (as preeminently embodied in the concept of formal sovereignty), and fraternity (solidarity of the people as a people rising above internal differences, solidarity as a people with other similarly oppressed peoples). The similarity of these objectives led many to call nationalist movements social movements too. However, the long history of political quarrel between workers' movements and nationalist movements indicates that we should retain two terms.

The objectives again were not new. But the French Revolution impressed on the world-system two concepts which had not been widely acknowledged previously. It took the concept of sovereignty, critical to the functioning of the interstate system which was the political superstructure of the capitalist world-economy, and transformed it from something invested in a "sovereign" into something invested in a "people." Secondly, it took an idea which had been applied up to then to only a very few states and made it the common property of all peoples, even those whose existence was as yet formally unacknowledged. It did this, curiously enough, not only by the spread of revolutionary ideals, in consonance, across frontiers, but also by the very imperialism of French revolutionary universalism in its Napoleonic guise, which stimulated an anti-French nationalism justified by the French Revolution itself. This phenomenon has made visible the two-faced character of modern nationalism, revolutionary vis-à-vis stronger, oppressive forces, but often imperialist in its turn, thereby always stimulating and legitimating further struggles.

Of course, as we know, the French Revolution was followed by the Restoration. The social movement was thought to be suppressed, and first of all in France, by the recreation of a monarchy, and both the social and national movements were presumably held in check, there and everywhere else, by Metternich's Concert of Europe. But it clearly was not to be so easy to put the genie back in the bottle. The sentiments that inspired both the social and the national movements continued to spread in multiple forms. The working class proto-movements of the first half of the nineteenth century contained all the key elements that would remain a part of the package ever since: organization (the secret societies in England, forced to be secret because of the Anti-Combination Laws); the attempts at collective "utopias" (advocated in varying forms by Owenites, Saint-Simonians, Fourierists); violence (Luddism and Blanquism to be sure, but also the Haitian Revolution and in particular its slave-led component); and demands upon the state for legislative reforms (campaign for an eight-hour day and against child and woman's labor, and of course Chartism in general, but also the campaign for Catholic emancipation both in Ireland and Great Britain).

Similarly, the expressions of nationalism in this period brought to light all the ambiguities that would continue to plague such movements later. New states would be created on the basis of "colonial" administrative boundaries (Latin American states, but also Belgium in 1830), led by groups able to profit from support generated by internal social unrest (the onward ideological thrust of the French Revolution) and a favorable international conjuncture (tacit or active support of one or more great powers against others), without necessarily mobilizing large sectors of internal lower strata.

In addition, the incorporation of new zones into the capitalist world-economy involved their political restructuring as well as a series of modern "states." This could take three different forms, as illustrated by the example of what happened to the Ottoman Empire. One form was nationalism per se, such as the Greek Revolution of the 1820s, which was overtly supported by Great Britain, represented, in prototypical fashion, by both that early "third worldist" romantic liberal, Lord Byron, and that quintessential cultural imperialist, Lord Elgin. A second form was reforming reconstruction from within: the "breakaway" of Egypt from the Ottoman Empire, led by the first of the "modernizers," Muhammed Ali, whose efforts gave rise to such ambiguous responses by Great Britain and France. They favored Ali's efforts when these efforts weakened the Sublime Porte (and especially when the Sublime Porte was acting against their interests) and opposed Ali's efforts when they threatened to create a really strong Egyptian state. The third form was reforming reconstruction from without: the conquest of Algeria in 1830 by the French (and eventually its colonization), which gave rise to an immediate reactive movement, later to be considered the origin of modern Algerian nationalism, the rebellion of Abd-el-Kader.

These first organizational expressions of the period following the French Revolution were confused, as might well be expected. Groups tried what they could, without too much intellectual analysis or discussion of strategy. It would be the general revolutionary ambiance of 1848–49 and its political failures that would provoke this analysis and this discussion.

In terms of the social movement, the 1848 Revolution in France marked the first time that a proletarian-based political group made a serious attempt to achieve political power and legitimize workers' power (legalization of trade unions, control of the workplace). The attempt was resisted fiercely, a short but intense civil war broke out (June days in Paris), and order was recreated in the form of military dictatorship with some populist overtones (Bonapartism). What 1848 in France demonstrated was that it would be no simple matter for the social movement to achieve its objectives. It was no accident that Marx's most famous concrete political analysis was the one he made of these very events in *The Eighteenth Brumaire*. Nor was it any accident that the primary strategic document of the modern social movement (and the most influential one), the *Communist Manifesto*, was published in 1848. It was published, to be sure, just before the June days, and indeed written during the year preceding, but it was the lesson of the June days that ensured that what might otherwise have become an obscure pamphlet of a minuscule group gave rise to a world movement.

The lesson of 1848 was not a lesson only for the social movement; 1848 was also the "springtime of the nations," a springtime that seemed all too brief. The attempts in various countries (most notably in Germany, Italy, and Hungary) to create new sovereign states, on the basis of constitutionalism and nationalist claims, were in fact soundly defeated largely because, unlike in the earlier cases of Greece, Belgium, or the Latin American states, the international conjuncture was no longer favorable. This did not mean that, in an unfavorable conjuncture, any national movement was automatically doomed. What it did make clear is that national revolution, like social revolution, was no simple matter, that one had to count first of all on one's own strength, and that this strength had to be sedulously created over time.

Hence for both the social and the national movements, the primary lesson to be drawn from the experience of 1848 was the need for *long-term* political organization as the necessary tool with which their objectives might be achieved. This lesson was well learned; some might say even too well. It became the strategic axiom of all significant movements ever since that time.

This decision, for it was a decision, was not made lightly, nor without due consideration. Indeed, for the social movement, it was the question which dominated its discussions between 1848 and 1870, the next dramatic historic date, that of the Paris Commune. The form that this debate took was quite open. It was one between the Marxists and the Anarchists within the International Working Men's Association (the First International, founded in 1862) on the one hand, and between Marxists and the Proudhonists in European working-class circles in general.

Basically, the Proudhonists hoped to achieve working-class objectives by withdrawal from capitalist production and the Anarchists by destroying the state which they saw as the pillar of the capitalist system. The heart of the opposing Marxist position on political strategy is well-known. Withdrawal, on the one hand, was an inefficacious strategy and in any case was self-indulgent and not progressive. Destruction of the state, on the other hand, was no easy task. The alternative to both that the Marxists suggested was the organized pursuit of the acquisition of state power based on the revolutionary potential of those who had "nothing to lose but their chains." The latter was identified quite specifically as the industrial proletariat. The emphasis on collective organization led to the depreciation of anything that seemed "individualistic." The ethic of work was not to be rejected but to be used by the only persons truly ready to employ it in the service of the general good. Both withdrawal and anti-statism were not merely incorrect strategies; they were also stances too readily transmutable into Bohemianism, which could easily deteriorate into attitudes associated with the irresponsible and politically dangerous lumpenproletariat. Social transformation was to be the consequence of sober, socially conscious effort.

The Paris Commune was thus in many senses a surprise. It was not in fact the result of planned effort. Its organization was very much the result of a particular political conjuncture, the defeat of France by Germany. It was to be sure crushed by military force, the result of a Franco-German class alliance of ruling strata. But it provided for the first time evidence for the ability of the working classes, in a revolutionary situation, to organize themselves fast and efficiently, to mobilize mass support, and to be socially inventive. It thus gave concrete meaning to the concept of a (temporary) "dictatorship of the proletariat" and ensured long life to this critical concept. In 1872, the Marxist position within the First International was finally officially accepted, as against the Bakuninist (Anarchist) position. But the First International, essentially a weak collection of weak movements, would die within four years. So would most of the weak movements. Their place was taken in most west European countries by serious, national working-class parties and serious national trade-union federations, which would form the basis of a new Second International.

From 1870 to World War I, the issue of political organization having been resolved, the internal debate of the social movement, which had now become the socialist movement, revolved around three principal problems.

(1) Most European states came now to have not one but two national working-class structures—a trade-union federation, and a socialist or labor political party. The two structures were supported by essentially the same people and had overlapping leadership, but for the most part they were distinct structures with different primary arenas of action. The trade unions were designed to function in the workplace and in the larger "economy." Their main efforts were directed at obtaining for the workers from the capitalist entrepreneurs what they considered their due. Their main weapons were on the one hand the strike, the attempt to pressure capitalists by halting their production and thereby their profits and, on the other hand, negotiations, either directly or via political authorities. The political parties were designed to function in the state structures and in the wider "political" arena. Their main efforts were also directed to obtaining what they considered to be the due of the working classes, but this time from the state. Their main weapons were analogous to those of the trade

unions. They could "strike" (that is, use a sort of violence) against the state authorities or they could negotiate with them.

With the same presumed objectives, the same presumed mass support, and an analogous range of weapons, one might have thought that their efforts would have been synchronous. However, with two structures, the question of hierarchical priority inevitably arose. This was immediately complicated by the fact that two social tendencies (or "deviations") emerged which tended to be unequally distributed between the two types of organizations.

The first tendency was the emergence of what was pejoratively called the "aristocracy of labor." This controversial term presumably referred to the fact that the more skilled workers who were better paid were often more politically "conservative" in the policies they advocated, reflecting their "class position," the fact that they did in fact have more to lose than their chains. But it was precisely among such workers that the trade-union movement first took hold, and retrospectively it seems almost inevitable that such workers played a disproportionate role in the leadership of the trade-union movement. Over time, this meant that trade-union demands moved in a "bread-and-butter" direction. The second tendency was that party membership began to reflect an evolving trans-class alliance. In particular the party of the working classes attracted an intelligentsia of bourgeois origin and often of continuing occupational location in middle and upper strata. Such persons, precisely because of their class background, often had more training than workers in the organizational skills needed by a political party. Over time, many parties came to utilize such "intellectuals" in ever-increasing number, and many of the latter saw the party as a mechanism of the "avant-garde" designed to contain the "syndicalism" of the "labor aristocracy."

(2) The seeds of contradiction were sown in this period. Although they did not then take the form of open internal conflict, merely that of a strain over the hierarchical priority of party and trade union, this contradiction has never been overcome. Rather, it became integral to, though not identical with, the second great internal difference of opinion within the socialist movement. This was the question of what tactics would permit the achievement of state power. Put briefly, the choice was to be posed as evolutionary parliamentarism versus revolutionary insurrection. This debate was originally conducted in good faith among comrades, this is to say, among persons sharing the same objective of achieving a socialist society.

It was forced upon the movement by a simple social reality which was beyond their control, the slow but continuous extension of the suffrage, particularly in the core countries of the capitalist world-economy. The movement to extend suffrage had long been a demand for democratization, but somewhere in the middle of the nineteenth century, it occurred to conservative forces that it might be used as a marvelous mechanism of cooptation. This is symbolized by the fact that it was the Tory Disraeli and not the Liberal Gladstone who proposed the most dramatic extension of suffrage in Great Britain (as indeed it was the conservative Bismarck in Germany who *de facto* invented the idea of welfare state).

The extension of suffrage forced upon the socialist parties the question of whether to participate in elections, whether to participate in parliament, and by the late nineteenth century whether to participate in government. There were those who saw no good reason not to do so, especially (they noted) since their electorate was, almost by definition, the majority of the population and, hence, it was the socialist parties who would be likely to be the great beneficiaries of universal suffrage. The state would "evolve" in a socialist direction. In opposition, the skeptics argued what had been previously argued by all the Marxists vis-à-vis the Proudhonists and the Bakuninists, that matters were not as simple as that. The governing bourgeoisie would not permit itself to be blithely voted out of power, or more exactly they would not permit an electoral destruction of capitalism. They would resist, in multiple ways, and hence the proletariat had to prepare itself for a hard conflict, a "revolution."

Still, in Western Europe (and North America), the "revisionist" doctrine of "evolutionary socialism" was very seductive. It seemed to offer immediate, concrete results. It seemed in fact less "utopian" than tactics that involved insurrection or armed struggle. And as the parties developed into mass parties, this perspective gained ever greater strength, both among the militants and among the leadership. It was indeed only in Russia, where there were scarcely any parliamentary elections, and only a small industrial proletariat, that "revisionism" seemed less plausible. In 1902, in the great split within the Russian Social-Democratic Party, the antirevisionists gained control of the party structure. The "Bolsheviks" under Lenin argued that only an underground party of cadres (as opposed to an open mass party) had any chance of achieving power. Given the tsarist state, Lenin's argument was not only plausible; it was highly pragmatic.

Behind the evolutionary vs. revolutionary, Menshevik vs. Bolshevik quarrel lay two analytical equivocations in the heart of Marxist analysis.

The first was the tension between determinism and voluntarism. Marx essentially tried to pursue a middle path concerning this old metaphysical conundrum of Western thought. He tended to argue voluntarism against bourgeois liberalism, and determinism against rival socialist thinkers. In general, his dominant tone was determinist. The revisionists picked up on this theme and used it to argue the "inevitability" of evolutionary socialism, which thereupon justified a politics of incrementalism. In response to this, Leninism was clearly more on the voluntarist side, arguing the crucial importance of decisive, planned action by a dedicated and informed minority.

The second equivocation in Marxist analysis was the debate about consciousness. For Marx, consciousness was a superstructure which reflected its economic base, but this was not, could not be, a simple one-to-one correlation, since there could be "false consciousness." How then could one determine the truth of a given consciousness? One way might be to let history decide, that is, to assume that over time men come to adjust their consciousness spontaneously such that it becomes a true reflection of their material reality. The second way might be to anticipate and accelerate history, permitting those with political insight to guide others. The first view was clearly more consonant with the revisionist path. The second demanded the Bolshevik path, that of the creation of an avant-garde cadre party. It is clear too how this was linked to the two tendencies discussed above, that of the increasing role of an "aristocracy of labor" on the one hand, with a need to assert that their evolving consciousness was a true, long-term reflection of their material base, and that of "revolutionary intellectuals" (often of bourgeois origin), with a need to argue that their evolving consciousness was a correct interpretation of the material base of the working class, as opposed to the short-run, syndicalist interpretations that were so widespread.

(3) The third problem was the relationship of socialists to nationalism on the one hand and to peasant demands on the other. This is usually presented as two separate intellectual issues, and indeed they were argued separately at the time. But they were in fact part of a single debate, the debate of the role in the process of the struggle for socialism of all those who were not industrial proletarians, and indeed industrial proletarians coming from the majority (or dominant) ethnic group of a given state. The "others" could be called a "minority" ethnic group or a "nation" demanding national rights—minimally cultural rights, maximally political rights, always more economic equality. Or the "others" could be the rural work-

ing population, expressing their grievances, demanding to retain the fruits of their labor, which often was expressed by a demand to own the land they toiled.

Once again, the socialist movement has two different reactions to these claims. One reaction was to deny the legitimacy of the demands of these "others." Capitalism, it was argued, was a process which over time would homogenize the world, eliminating thereby both "nations" and "peasants" as categories. Therefore, it was futile and dangerous to slow down this process by advocating the rights of any group other than that of the industrial proletariat. Such advocacy simply divided the working class. This proposition was quite consonant in fact with evolutionary socialism. The alternative position at this time was not the obverse one of *full* support either for "nationalist" claims or for "peasant" claims, for that would have betrayed the basic internationalist, workerist commitment of Marxist ideology. The alternative position was rather that of asserting the legitimacy of an *interim* alliance between the working class and the "others," based on the fact that these "others" were also oppressed by the same ruling strata, but an alliance that was only tactical and under the "hegemony" of the working class. Such hegemony, however, was only possible if there were an avant-garde cadre party to exercise it. It was, therefore, a view that only made sense within a Leninist perspective, and indeed it became the Leninist position. It is curious, but revealing, to observe that when World War I began, the revisionists, who had rejected "nationalism" so strongly, emerged as exponents of the sacred national *alliance* within their respective states, while the Leninists, who had been willing to consider tactical alliances with "nationalists," emerged as the upholders of an internationalist rejection of the legitimacy of bourgeois nationalist war.

The great expansion of the organized working-class movements of Europe from 1870 to 1914 took place at the same time as, and within the context of, the last great imperial territorial expansion of Europe in modern history. Therefore, at the very moment the socialist movements were seeking to find their way as antisystemic movements emphasizing anticapitalism, there emerged nationalist movements in the periphery, seeking to find their way as antisystemic movements emphasizing anti-imperialism. The nationalist movements went through the same debate about the centrality of political organization as a strategy, as had the socialist movements, with perhaps a twenty to thirty year lag. For nationalism, the equivalent of the Proudhonist *cum* Anarchist position was that of so-called cultural nationalism, a tendency which argued the necessity of a withdrawal from the dominating society through cultural renaissance and the cultivation of linguistic, artistic, and behavioral self-assertion and separation. The political nationalists argued, analogously to the position of the Marxists vis-à-vis the Proudhonists and Anarchists, that cultural nationalism was impossible at best, deceptive and false at worse, since an autonomy that was not guaranteed by control of a state apparatus did not have the material base to survive. The conquest of state power, in this case usually via secession and/or the creation of a new state entity, became then the prime strategic objective, and to this end the creation of a "party" structure was indispensable.

The intellectual parallel among nationalists to the revisionist-Leninist debate among socialists was the debate over the method by which political nationalist objectives could be achieved. At one end were those who advocated the path of "constitutionalism," that is, the negotiation with existing authorities of a step-by-step transfer of power to the national group in question. At the opposed end were those who spoke of more militant methods that involved mass mobilization, conflict, and protracted (and, if necessary, violent) struggle. It should be noted, however, that if, theoretically, Marxism started out as a movement committed to revolutionary struggle and only over time developed a stronger and stronger "revisionist" component involving parliamentarianism as a tactic, political nationalism in country after country (India, China, the Arab world, Mexico, South Africa) started out as a predominantly constitutionalist movement and only over time developed a stronger and stronger "revolutionary" component.

The two different trajectories were a function of the geographical loci and therefore the class composition of the two groups of movements at that earlier point in historic time. The socialist movements were to be found largely in core countries, the nationalist movements largely in peripheral ones. The socialist movements began as structures whose political base was in the industrial proletariat and which later extended their bases of support by appealing to the anticapitalist (and in non-core countries anti-imperialist) sentiments of the broad masses of the population. The nationalist movements began as structures whose social base was in peripheral bourgeoisies and intelligentsias and which later extended their bases of support by appealing to the anti-imperialist sentiments of the broad masses of the population. As each broadened the class alliance that underlay the movement, a phenomenon that derived from the basic decision to give strategic priority to the conquest of state power, the tactics of the two sets of movements began to converge.

As the political nationalist movements broadened their base, the quarrel they had with cultural nationalists began to diminish. As long as the nationalist movements were small committees of bourgeois and intelligentsia seeking constitutional change, they could preach one variety or another of cultural integration or "Westernization." This could take the form of outright adoption of Western cultural premises (language, religion, dress, etc.) or the same thing in edulcorated form (for example, the reinterpretation of Islam or Hinduism or Confucianism to demonstrate that "modern" values were not exclusively "Western" or "Christian" but were already inherent in and expressed by the traditional literature). When, however, these movements began to seek mass support, it was no longer plausible to preach assimilation. Quite the contrary; for the mass of the population, anti-imperialism had to mean the preservation and reassertion of what was theirs against that which appertained to the conqueror. Conversely, as revolutionary social movements broadened their base, they had to talk more in terms of the "people" as a whole rather than just the "working class" and this logically led them to sound more "nationalist."

The political nationalist movements, as they became more militant, became more culturally nationalist. There was, however, a limit, because the political nationalist movements, being political, operated within the constraints of the political system of states. Here too there was a convergence with the Marxists. As the Leninist wing of Marxism moved toward a *limited* recognition of the legitimacy of nationalist (that is, in its eyes, cultural) objectives, so the political nationalist movements sought to maintain a middle position combining national political objectives, class political objectives, and cultural objectives. The ground was being laid for a new political analysis. The Russian Revolution was the fundamental catalyst for the new developments. Russia in 1917 was both the most "backward" of the industrial countries and the most "advanced" of the non-core countries. We are less surprised today than everyone was at the time that it was Russia, not Germany (or England), in which took place the revolution, the "ten days that shook the world." The Russian Revolution shook the world-system not just because it was the first successful revolution under the banner of Marxism but even more because it occurred where it did. Socialists throughout the world had expected the first revolution to occur in Germany, largely because, in the period from 1870 on, the strongest socialist movement (strongest in terms of national political support, strongest in terms of intellectual force) was that of Germany. When, then, revolution occurred first in Russia, it was natural to interpret this at first as an "accident" which would soon be rectified by a German revolution.

But the German revolution failed, and indeed failed decisively. Within a few years, this was recognized by everyone. Lenin drew the sensible tactical conclusion: if not Germany, then the "Orient." It was at the Congress of Baku in 1921 that Lenin in effect proposed a formal alliance between the anticapitalist social movements of the core and the anti-imperialist nationalist movements of the periphery. Such an alliance, however, involved extraordinary ambiguities with whose consequences we are still living today. The Russian Revolution "proved" to the world that a revolution could occur, and eventually it would prove that a revolutionary state could industrialize and transform itself in military and political strength. But what exactly did that in turn prove? How was that different (was it different?) from the proof already made in 1905 that a non-European state (Japan) could defeat militarily a European state (in that case Russia)? Both "proofs" served to transform the social psychology of revolutionary movements, offering them the basis for the fundamental optimism of will that has been a pillar of their political strength ever since. But both proofs also opened up the question of exactly what was revolutionary about the revolution.

In fact, as we know, the counteroffensive of the world's dominant forces against the Bolshevik state meant that the USSR turned neither toward Germany nor toward the Orient but rather turned inward toward "socialism in one country," toward the defense of the USSR as a beleaguered state. The control of state power may not have been enough to transform the Soviet Union. But it was certainly enough to transform the Third International from a network of parallel movements into a hierarchical structure adjusted to the needs of a particular state power. The question thereupon became what role the Third International and thus the USSR would play as an antisystemic force within the world-system. From 1920 or so until the outbreak of World War II, the answer was very uncertain. On the one hand, the rivalries and maneuvers among the "leading" capitalist powers that had given rise to World War I were unabated and would eventually lead to a World War II. Furthermore, as we know, the eventual division into two military blocs would take on strong ideological clothing, as a struggle between a "liberal" coalition and a "fascist" one. Was this to be regarded, as Lenin had regarded the 1914 war, as a struggle among thieves, or was there a choice between a greater and a lesser danger?

The actual tactical decisions were made by the Third International in parallel form in the center and in the periphery. The prime cases, which served as models in each sector, were those of Germany and China. In Germany, the question was whether the Communist Party should enter into a "popular front" (as it came to be called later) with the Second International Social-Democrats against the right, and especially against the Nazis, or whether instead they should think of Social-Democrats as "social fascists." In China, the question was whether the Communist Party should maintain its tactical alliance with the Kuomintang against world imperialist forces, and especially against Japan, or whether it should give priority to civil war. Neither question was ever answered clearly. The Third International shifted gears several times, the local Communist parties as well (the party in China somewhat less in consonance with the Soviet Union's shifts than the party in Germany). And of course, the question would repeat itself everywhere else—in Spain and in India, for example.

Behind the uncertainties of Third International policy in the interwar years lay a deeper question of the kind of alliance implied by Baku. For, as would become clear after 1945, a political alliance between socialist parties in the core and anti-imperialist movements in the periphery could in fact have two quite different implications. It could be a way by which certain middle strata in both segments of the world-system could be incorporated into the spoils of the system, under the ideological cover of a new order; or it could be a bringing together of two different antisystemic families into one, far more powerful single family, which would then truly have the weight to transform the system as a whole. If this question was not simply or straightforwardly answered then or since, it is because of certain contradictory trends within the capitalist world-economy itself. The extension and deepening over time of the capitalist process within the capitalist world-economy had extended and deepened the polarization of classes on a world scale, and thereby strengthened the social base of antisystemic movements. This same process, however, had also reinforced the geographical emphasis, the "spatialization" of class polarization, and thereby reduced even further the parallelism of the political processes in the various states. This had diminished the likelihood of trans-state intermovement alliances, giving the world's bourgeoisie precious weapons of control and reward.

The extension and deepening over time of the capitalist process within the capitalist world-economy had furthermore extended and deepened the role of the states and the interstate system as key institutions. This had made the control of state power all the more important, while simultaneously making it less useful, at least in the weaker states. Hence state power as an antisystemic weapon had become ambiguous. It could be used to undermine the system but its acquisition by antisystemic movements had given them a stake in supporting the framework of the interstate system. In the post-1945 period this dilemma would begin to play itself out.

2. Postwar Success of the Movements: Triumphs and Ambiguities

People resist exploitation. They resist as actively as they can, as passively as they must. The period from 1789 to 1945 had involved a long odyssey of difficult organizing. It had been an uphill struggle, during which the majority of the people in the world felt greatly oppressed. 1945 in this sense represented a psychological turning point. Success for the world's antisystemic movements now seemed for the first time within reach. The strategy adopted in the nineteenth century seemed about to pay off. That strategy, let us remember, involved a sequence, a simple sequence but a sequence nonetheless: first mobilize to attain state power, then utilize state power to transform society (in the direction of liberty, equality, fraternity).

We have come, in the years since 1945, to talk of three "worlds"—the industrialized Western world (which has been taken to mean primarily Western Europe, North America, and Australasia; but since circa 1970 also Japan); the socialist countries (the usual list is the USSR, Eastern Europe, China, [North] Korea, the three Indochinese states, and also Cuba); the so-called third world (the three continents of Asia, Africa, and Latin America). The boundary lines have not always been clear. Furthermore, in terms of analyzing the operations of the world-economy and the interstate system, this tripartite division has often obscured more than it revealed. But this mode of political classification turns out, on closer look, to be useful in fact in terms of analyzing the antisystemic movements. The West is the region in which in most cases the primary heir of the nineteenth-century antisystemic movements is a "social-democratic" party, either one linked to the Second International, or another party which can be seen to be playing an analogous role. The socialist countries are, virtually by definition, those in which a party of Third International traditions is in power. The third world is a grouping where the primary mass representative of antisystemic traditions has been a nationalist or a national liberation movement.

This is not a question of ideological credentials. It is a question of which movement has been in fact able to mobilize politically the popular masses for a "struggle" against those with privilege (however labeled), which has found significant resonance for claims that it represents "popular" interests. Furthermore, not only did these three varieties of movements succeed in mobilizing popular support, albeit each primarily in one zone, but each variety has also succeeded during the post-1945 period in achieving its interim political objective—obtaining state power—in most of the states in its zone. Thus, one might say that the post-1945 period has been the period of success for these movements. They have fought well and they have triumphed. The problem has been that the triumph in each case has turned out to be ambiguous in its meaning. Let us analyze the triumphs and the ambiguities, zone by zone.

The social profile of the core countries of the world-system was in many ways fundamentally different in the post-1945 period than it had been, say, in 1850. The basic changes are familiar to us all. The concentration of the world's accumulated capital in these zones had meant that over all the mass standard of living had risen—not only for the educated professionals or cadres but also for the skilled and semi-skilled working classes. There did remain a very poor underclass, but even they had become smaller in overall percentage of the national population. In addition, they had become usually more clearly identifiable as an ethnically distinctive group. In many cases, these latter lacked formal citizenship rights, being designated "migrants." Consequently, whereas in 1850 perhaps 80–90 percent of a given state's population might have been classified as very "poor," the percentage in 1950 was nearer to one-third. The same could be said of the degree to which the population was "educated." In 1850, at most 10 percent finished secondary school, by 1950 at least two-thirds did so. Furthermore, the population had become highly urbanized, and those working in rural areas (still a majority in 1850) were now reduced to a quite small percentage of the population. Thus, in the post-1945 period, the traditional "peasantry" of these countries had either disappeared or was fast fading as a numerically significant group.

The overall wealth of the core countries was matched, at least by the post-1945 period, by the institutionalization of a relatively liberal political system, based at last upon universal suffrage (although still not including "migrants"). These states had multi-party systems which everywhere tended to move in the direction of a predominantly two-party system: one party more or less "conservative," the other more or less "social-democratic." Neither of the two parties was normally entirely class-based, but the "social-democratic" party had a strong base in the working classes.

In 1945, however, this now familiar profile, seemed still to rest on very shaky foundations, from the point of view of the working classes and their movements. The experience of the depression of 1929 was just behind them as well. Neither a higher standard of living nor a liberal constitutional structure seemed secure, or even yet achieved in some cases. Above all, as of 1945, the working classes of these countries had the sense that every gain they have made (whether suffrage, or access to education, or shorter work hours, or social welfare) had been fought for very strenuously, at very great cost, and that these gains remained therefore tenuous.

The working classes felt, in short, that they had been engaged in a difficult class struggle, and that they still suffered not only from economic denial but from social exclusion. Above all, they did not feel as though they had *droit de cité* in the political structures of the state. Thus in 1945 the critical struggle was still considered to be ahead of them. What changed subsequently in the post-1945 period was that, in one country after another, the working-class movement came to feel that the key battle had now occurred and that they had in some sense won it. Often this took the form simply of winning a major electoral battle: Labour's victory in 1945 in Great Britain, Mitterand's election in France in 1981, the first Social-Democratic government in the Federal Republic of Germany. The ability of labor to impose itself as a central institutional pillar of Democratic Party politics in the United States in the 1940s served as a social-psychological equivalent. Perhaps the same thing could be said of the Belgian Socialist Party's role in the abdication of King Leopold. In all the Nordic countries and the Netherlands, the labor parties solidly ruled for long periods. Spain, Portugal, and Greece more or less joined these ranks in the 1980s. Italy is perhaps an exception. The only remaining Western country where the mass workers' movement is still represented by a Communist party seems not yet to have had an equivalent catharsis. The *compromesso storico* had been intended to serve as that, and some might argue that the control of regional governments by the PCI for so long has had the same impact. Japan is perhaps also a second partial exception. In general, however, in each country, by the 1980s the coming to power of working-class movements (via an electoral path, to be sure) was no longer ahead of them (as had been true for the most part in 1945) but behind them.

A somewhat parallel scenario occurred in that band of countries from the Elbe to East Asia we have called the socialist countries. The Russian Revolution of 1917 was a seizure of power by force. It was therefore a revolution and was felt to be one by its supporters and its enemies. It was furthermore a revolution conducted on the particular model that we have come to call "Marxist-Leninist." This model comprised two key elements, one for each successive phase. For the phase of mobilization, it involved the creation of an avant-garde party of cadres dedicated to the seizure of power. For the period after the seizure of power, it involved a "dictatorship of the proletariat" in which power remained exclusively in the hands of this same avant-garde party of cadres.

In 1917, nonetheless, the Bolsheviks were surprised by their own success and at first thought their power could not endure without a successful German revolution. While they soon gave up this prospect as a chimera, they continued to feel insecure because of the country's encirclement by hostile powers, a fear that culminated in the reality of the German invasion in 1941 and the extreme devastation of the war. But in 1945, they had in fact survived the invasion and won the war, and there seems little reason to doubt that then at last the Communist Party of the Soviet Union felt that it was securely in power and would stay there.

In the immediate postwar period, Communist governments came to power in eight countries in East-Central Europe, and also in China and in the northern half of Korea. In three of these countries—China, Yugoslavia, and Albania—this was made possible primarily by the fact that during World War II armed resistance forces led by the country's Communist Party emerged as the strongest military and political force in the country. Thus this coming to power was effectuated by a Marxist-Leninist party that had succeeded in incarnating nationalism and thereby leading a successful battle against a foreign invader. In the seven other countries, the situation was different. There seems little doubt that, were it not for the presence of Soviet troops in these countries in the post-1945 period, the various Communist parties might never have come to power at all, or might never have been able to stay there very long. Still, even in these countries, the Communist party had grown stronger because of the war. The situation of course varied country by country. Thus, at least for part of the working class, there was a sense that the working class had seized power and could therefore now proceed to "construct socialism."

Finally, in the three great continents—Asia, Africa, and Latin America—which we came in the post-1945 period to group together as the "third world" or the "South," this period was the period of "decolonization." It was also the period of "Bandung," that is, of the assertion of the collective political presence in the world-system of this group of countries or peoples. This entire zone had been the object of a continuing "expansion of Europe" since the sixteenth century, that culminated in the last third of the nineteenth century in the colonization (or the semi-colonization) of virtually the whole non-European world. This colonization was of course resisted in multiple ways and, in one country after another, whether a formal colony or nominally still independent, there arose movements to end oppression, to liberate peoples, to liberate the people. Generically we call these movements "nationalist" in the sense that sooner or later the predominant ideological theme of such movements came to be the rights of a people, a "nation," to self-government and to be considered the equal of any other people.

The attempts to create political movements which had a solid "popular" base and were therefore politically significant was one that was opposed in every way by the various colonial (or imperialist) powers. But eventually, in one country after another, such movements emerged and usually incorporated within their nationalist rhetoric a social rhetoric as well. The degree to which they were able to mobilize mass support was often a function of the degree to which they seemed to stand not only for the liberty and equality of peoples, but for liberty and equality among the people.

In a formal colony, the political objective of mobilization seemed clear—the achievement of independence. In the "semi-colonies," countries that were formally independent, the immediate political objective seemed closer to that defined by working-class movements in the nineteenth century—the coming to power of a truly antisystemic movement, in this case, a genuinely "nationalist" movement. Such a coming to power represented a nationalist "catharsis" of the "popular classes" quite analogous to that felt by the "working classes" when they finally won *droit de cité*, either by electoral or insurrectionary means. Before 1945, there were very few such nationalist catharses in the three continents (perhaps the Mexican Revolution, and the Atatürk period in Turkey). After 1945, there were very many. In Asia, they were for the most part rapid, because of the history of Japanese expansion and Japanese defeat during World War II. China and Korea, already mentioned, were of course part of this upsurge. But all of Southeast Asia now became independent: the Philippines, Indonesia, Burma, Malaysia and the three Indochinese states—Vietnam, Laos, Cambodia. And the Indian subcontinent, although not actually invaded by Japan, gained independence as well in 1948.

In most of these cases, the drive for independence was led by a movement with genuine popular support and a history of struggle. Despite what might be thought of as the favorable geopolitical conjuncture, independence had to be fought for, up to the very last minute. The nationalist movements felt that it was this struggle that had enabled them to obtain power. Certainly, this was the case for the two giants—India and Indonesia. In this sense one can surely think of this coming to power as providing a nationalist catharsis based on a feeling of political triumph. The Indochinese states were special in that in these countries the nationalist movements that came to power were simultaneously Marxist-Leninist movements, which was not true elsewhere in South and Southeast Asia. Undoubtedly, the very long military struggle (almost thirty years in the case of Vietnam) was a major factor in explaining this coupling.

In the Arab Machrek, where most states were nominally independent, the form was somewhat different. But it can be argued that the Nasser government in Egypt and the original coming to power of the Baath in Syria and Iraq created a sense of popular triumph, of nationalist catharsis. In North Africa, formally colonized, the coming to power of the Neo-Destour in Tunisia, of Istiqlal in Morocco, and above all the Algerian National Liberation Front after a long military struggle, were similar nationalist triumphs.

In Black Africa, given the large number of separate political units, the story was complex. But there can be little doubt that there was the sense that a "downward thrust of African liberation" had occurred beginning in the 1950s, in which such early movements as the Convention Peoples Party in the Gold Coast, the RDA in French-speaking Africa, KANU in Kenya and TANU in Tanganyika, the MPLA in Angola and Frelimo in Mozambique, and SWAPO in Namibia—as well as of the African National Congress (ANC) still struggling in South Africa today—incarnated this same popular demand for liberty and equality, and their coming to power was celebrated as a great popular triumph.

Latin America is no doubt a special story. Other than in the Caribbean, the Latin American states had become independent in the early nineteenth century, on the basis of nationalist movements led by European settlers (as in British North America), after which most of these countries fell into a long period of relative political stagnation. Thus in the twentieth century it was not fully clear whether they should have been thought of (and should have thought of themselves) as equivalent to European states faced with a "workers (socialist) movement" demanding power, or equivalent to the semi-colonial states of Asia and Africa faced with a "popular (nationalist) movement" demanding power. In Chile, the situation was perhaps closer to the former; in countries such as Peru, Mexico, and Cuba (with large non-White sectors of the population), it was perhaps closer to the latter.

In any case, in the post-1945 period, this sense of "coming to power" was certainly felt in Cuba and Nicaragua as it had earlier been felt in Mexico. It was felt in Allende's Chile but there the power was momentary. APRA came to power too late in Peru for quite such a catharsis. Whether the Vargas experience in Brazil (which began in the 1930s) and Peronism in Argentina had a similar impact is debatable. Certainly both Getulio Vargas and Juan Peron mobilized popular nationalist sentiment in important ways.

What this survey of the three "worlds" allows us to recognize is that the period after 1945, in at least a majority of the countries of the world, representing at least three-quarters of the world's population, the ostensible intermediate objective of nineteenth-century antisystemic movements—the coming to power either of a workers or of a popular movement—had in fact occurred. Furthermore, most people felt this was a great achievement, and most such regimes boasted about this achievement.

These political facts changed fundamentally the direction in which eyes were turned, shifting concern from what we can call stage one (the mobilization to obtain power) to stage two (using the power to bring about social transformation). If one compares the results of "coming to power" in the post-1945 of three types of movements—the "Social-Democrats" in the core (OECD, developed) countries, the communists in the "East," and the "nationalists" in the third world—what do we find? We find first of all that each kind of movement had one fundamental "reform" or change to its credit, one for which they claimed credit publicly, one which was indeed rightfully to their credit. The Social-Democrats claimed to have legislated the core countries into "welfare states"—that is, states in which the government created various kinds of social insurance structures. Simultaneously, they claimed to be responsible for negotiated increases in the real wage levels of at least skilled and semiskilled workers and of course of the professional cadres. This latter "social compromise" has been called "Fordism."

Social insurance programs and Fordism were not, to be sure, the doing of the Social-Democrats alone. Conservative forces eventually acceded to these reforms, appreciating correctly that, despite certain costs, the reforms were both cooptative politically and advantageous macro-economically.

Still, conservative forces acceeded as a *pis aller*, and almost always because they were under strong pressure from the working-class movements. It would be more exact to say that the reforms only occurred because of Social Democratic pressure but were largely retained when the Social-Democrats lost elections because the more conservative parties felt that there were some advantages in these changes as well as that their abolition would be very disruptive politically. Nonetheless, no doubt conservative forces always sought to whittle away at the welfare state and reduce real wages, and working class forces always had to fight back.

In the Communist countries, the great reform was the socialization of the means of production (including for the most part in agriculture), and the establishment of a state planning structure. This amounted to a sort of social insurance cum Fordism as well, but one at a lower absolute level than in the core countries though at a higher level of certainty (and particularly the certainty of employment). This permitted the great achievement of the socialist countries—a relatively rapid rate of industrialization.

By and large, in the countries of the third world, the coming to power of the "nationalists" has meant neither much social insurance nor much increase in real wages nor very much nationalization of the means of production (especially given the continuing quite large role of private transnational corporations in most of them). The great reform of the nationalist movements has been instead the indigenization of personnel—in the sphere of government to be sure, but to a very large extent in posts in the private economic sector also as well as in what might be called cultural positions.

The great reforms in each of the three zones of the post-1945 world were both meaningful and difficult to achieve. The movements had every right to feel proud of their accomplishments. They had struggled, and they had achieved. They expected applause and gratitude, and at first they received both.

All these "reforms" were internal to the countries. What the movements had promised in the realm of foreign policy was "international solidarity" with similar movements elsewhere not yet in power. Their actions in this domain were far less impressive than those in the domestic sphere. That is not to say that Social-Democrats in power did not support Social-Democrats not yet in power, or that Communists in power did not support Communists not yet in power, or that national liberation movements in power did not support national liberation movements not yet in power.

They often did, but not as often nor as unreservedly as one might have expected or as they claimed.

Furthermore, it was relatively rare for one kind of antisystemic movement in power in one country to support a different kind of antisystemic movement not yet in power in another country, even if the latter showed evidence of being a popular and antisystemic force. It seems clear that on the whole the three varieties of antisystemic movement tended to associate themselves primarily with other movements of the same type and to regard with some suspicion any instance of another kind of movement. There were to be sure individual and collective exceptions, but the overall tendency was to make the three "worlds" into three movement-cocoons.

There were many reasons for this, but two stand out in seeking an explanation of this pattern. One was movement history. The Social-Democrats and the Communists had a long history of bitter struggle, especially in Europe after 1917. The Communists and the national liberation movements had a very long history of mutual suspicion and misunderstanding, especially during the era of Stalin. And the Social-Democrats in the West tended to use the language of class struggle to oppose the claims of anticolonial movements, so that here too a long legacy of mutual suspicion and misunderstanding had been created.

The second reason was that of *raison d'état*. Movements in power found that they were governments of states, and that states have interests. Once one is in power, one major object is to stay in power, and this is dependent not merely on political forces located inside the country but also on political forces located outside it. International solidarity is an uplifting slogan, but for an antisystemic movement in power, the price could often be too high. And whenever it was, most movements pulled back. Not once but very often, Social-Democrats in power, Communists in power, national liberation movements in power have retreated very far from their solidarity obligations when they felt it necessary in order to safeguard their own survival. A fortiori this was true of Social-Democrats (and Communists sharing power in Western countries), when it came to dealing with anti-colonial movements in their own colonies.

Raison d'état pushed very far. The Social-Democrats got swept up, indeed became leaders of, the anticommunist crusade of the "free world." Communists, from the 1920s on, were swept up into the defense of the world's first and prime socialist country, the USSR, and consequently subordinated their actions to the needs of Soviet foreign policy. And national liberation movements in power found that a nonalignment that was more than mere rhetoric involved very costly and very immediate political and economic sacrifices, which few were able to afford for very long.

To be antisystemic is to argue that neither liberty nor equality is possible under the existing system and that both are possible only in a transformed world. Thus it seems quite understandable that the masses who mobilized to transform the world expected that, once the movements came to power, they would enjoy liberty and equality—if not in perfect measure, at least to a greater degree than previously. In general, it could be said that actual experience has been that the *initial* impact of coming to power has been exactly that—greater liberty and greater equality. But with time the situation changed until, in one country after another, there was acute disappointment (if not more) in the degree of liberty and equality actually realized. In some cases, the situation was even worse than before the coming to power.

If "liberty" has become a rhetorical concept which today is employed by both the left and right, "equality" remains a term still largely identified with the left. We should therefore expect the most notable actions in the realm of equality. Let us start with the most striking achievement in this realm which is to the credit of the movements in power. Everywhere, when the movements have come to power, there have been important advances in the availability of the two great "services" of the modern world—education and health. The extension of a "free" educational system (that is, one supported out of general taxes rather than user fees) and of a health system that was either "free" or based on relatively low-cost "insurance" has been one of the triumphs of the antisystemic movements of all kinds.

And yet, in practice, these advances have not eliminated inequalities. Rather, they have ameliorated some and hidden others. The basic issue is that there are endless possibilities to improve quality in these services, and therefore the positive consequences of their use. And since each improvement in quality represents a cost, there is an inherent social shortage. This means that there is a struggle for advantage, and some get better education and health than others, far better, even where the movements are in power. Whether the triage is through money, or through sophistication in ability to utilize the machinery of the services, or through special influence, the fact is that, despite all the advances in raising the threshold of available services, it is not at all clear that the gap between services available to the top strata and those available to the bottom strata has significantly narrowed as a result of the movements having taken power.

When one shifts from "services" (education and health, but also of course recreation and vacations) to what might be called "basics" (food, clothing, shelter), we find that the story is somewhat similar to the issue of services. There was an initial upsurge in benefits. Often, but not always, this upsurge has been maintained as a higher threshold level of benefits. But once again, it is not at all clear that the gap between the real income of the upper strata and the real income of the lower strata has been diminished, and in some cases it has even increased.

Finally, the least happy story has been in the realm of liberties. First of all, how have "minorities" fared in the countries where the movements have come to power? Social-Democratic movements have traditionally been ambiguous in their views of "minorities." Their traditional emphasis on the working class as a class led them to be suspicious of claims based on race or ethnicity or "nationality." They saw such claims as "divisive" of the working class. There were, however, two great pressures that pushed "Social-Democratic" movements out of their theoretical indifference to such issues. One was the fact that most such "minorities" in most countries have been a part (and a growing part) of the "working classes," and quite often its poorest and most oppressed sector. The logic of popular struggle demanded that Social-Democratic movements take positions on these "racial-ethnic" issues. The other pressure was the fact that right-wing movements in general (and in particular, neofascist ones) pushed overtly racist themes. And by rebound, if for no other reason, the Social-Democrats felt that they had to support the struggle of such "minorities." In power, however, we find the familiar pattern: some initial improvements—in such fields as immigration policy, control of police excesses, antidiscrimination legislation, affirmative action—but always up to a limit. The limit was usually that posed by the sense of the working-class "majority" of the potential competition of "minorities," a fear that of course was always made acute by economic recessions.

Has the picture been fundamentally different in the socialist countries? The USSR took a major step in the 1920s in recognizing the realities of ethno-national differences by reconstructing itself as a complex federation of nationally based units. In this way, each "group" was equal and had opportunities for the full "indigenization" of personnel and the use of the "national" language. At one level, this has worked remarkably well. But there have been "limits" here too. One limit has been the continuing fear of the central authorities of so-called bourgeois nationalism. The various separate ethno-national political units have been permitted indigenous personnel and language, provided that there was no difference in policies and no "chauvinism" (as defined by those in central control). In practice, this has meant a quadruple control—frequent political purges for "nationalist" excesses, the placement of the notorious number two in the apparatus who was almost always a Russian, the limitation of movement within the USSR which thereby maintained a spatial separateness, and the minimization of all ethno-national contact with those outside the frontiers of the USSR. The situation has involved even greater constraints or repressions for what might be called "suspect" nationalities—Jews, Crimean Tatars, Volga Germans, Ukrainians. This may however be changing now under Gorbachev.

Still, "federalism" has been a great achievement in the USSR. It has not been too widely emulated in fact in other socialist countries. Only Yugoslavia has a similar system, one indeed with even more national autonomy. Czechoslovakia and China have modified versions. In other socialist countries, "minorities" were given even less institutional autonomy, and pressures for "assimilation" have been more prominent.

The countries where national liberation movements of the third world have come to power have been even less tolerant of ethno-national minorities. They have seen the movements of these minorities not merely as divisive but as threatening to the national unity and to the ability of the movement to remain in power. Repression has often been quite swift.

If the picture of how "minorities" have fared in countries where movements have come to power tends to range from very bad to fair (rarely excellent), the story on personal liberties has been even more somber. The record of the socialist countries and those third world countries where movements have come to power has been not at all exemplary. The initial fears of genuine counterrevolutionary thrusts (often aided by outside forces) have generated a system wherein most persons were excluded from the process of real political debate, access to information was highly limited, no real control of abuses of bureaucratic power existed, and arbitrary and unjustified punishments were widespread. It is not merely that the liberties were few but that they were very unequally distributed.

Let us therefore sum up the experience of the post-1945 coming to power of the movements. Each kind of movement put into effect some very great reforms which have earned them substantial popular support. There were some great changes of which the movements could boast and whose consequences were visible. At the same time, despite initial advances in social equality, political liberty, and international solidarity, in the longer run, the movements disappointed, and disappointed greatly, in all three domains.

This has been observed widely. And to these accusations the movements in power essentially respond by three successive remarks. One, the great "reforms" are indeed fundamental and in themselves justify their historical record. Two, the limitations in equality, liberty, and solidarity are not their responsibility but the consequence of the difficulties imposed upon them by the defenders of the status quo. Three, if the movements persist (and come to power in still more countries) they will finally overcome the defenders of the status quo and will therefore finally realize fully what they have promised as social transformation. It is because many of the supporters of the antisystemic movements began to doubt this threefold response that the movements came into difficulties in the 1960s and since.

3. Forward to What? The Debate on Strategy Reopened

The year 1968 was as much of a symbolic turning point in the history of the movements as was 1848. The earlier year taught the movements the limitations and dangers of popular uprisings that were not adequately prepared. They drew from this experience the lesson that the movements had to become organizations with a long-term agenda, a centerpiece of which was the attainment of state power. By 1968, as we have argued, the "old" movements had by and large attained state power. The popular uprisings of 1968—in the United States, in France, in Italy, in Czechoslovakia, in Japan, in Mexico—were directed not merely against the existing world-system, the capitalist world-economy, but against the "old" antisystemic movements in power within this system. In the United States they occurred during the term of a Democratic president who had presided over the greatest extension of the welfare state and of civil rights for blacks in the history of the country. In France they occurred during the presidency of Charles DeGaulle who, if not incarnating social-democracy, was at least the symbol of anti-Nazi resistance and the political leader who had "decolonized" Algeria and Black Africa. In Czechoslovakia, the revolt was against the continuing reality of a Comintern imperial structure. In Mexico it was against the PRI, the party of an "institutionalized revolution" as its name reminds us.

The revolution of 1968 was a failure in the same sense and to the same degree as had been that of 1848. None of the rebelling groups obtained more than momentary acceptance of their immediate demands. It was a turning-point in the same sense and to the same degree as had been 1848. Those in control would forever after have to take account of and deal with the underlying popular demands of 1968. But, above all, 1968 had one crucial outcome. It launched a strategic debate among the movements in the same sense and to the same degree as had 1848. We know the outcome of the post-1848 debate. By the 1880s the movements had agreed on their basic *middle-run* strategy: they would seek to attain state power by political means. The revolution of 1968 challenged this nineteenth-century consensus on middle-run strategy. As a result, today we are in the midst of a renewed debate about middle-run strategy. It is not yet clear how and where this new debate will come out.

Let us start with the fact that the revolts of 1968 and the subsequent rise of "new" movements were primarily triggered by the sense that the "old" movements—the Social-Democrats, the Communists, the nationalists— had failed in many of their objectives, indeed had betrayed many of their objectives, and were in fact, as the expression went, "part of the problem, not part of the solution." The exact form of the complaint, however, took a somewhat different form in each of the three "worlds"—the core countries of the "West," the socialist countries of the "East," and the "third world." Because the form of the complaint was different and the kind of movement against which the complaint was made was different, the process gave rise in each zone to a somewhat different kind of "new" movement.

The context of the "confrontations" (as they came to be called) in the core countries came in the context of two central realities of the postwar world—the continuing wars of imperial power vs. movements of national liberation (most notably in Vietnam and Algeria), and the process of de-Stalinization of the world Communist movement (whose most spectacular event was Nikita Khruschchev's speech at the Twentieth Party Congress).

On the one hand, the wars against the national liberation movements conducted by or supported by the "Social-Democratic" movements of the West did not merely seem incongruous with their professed antisystemic objectives. They came in fact to dominate the national political horizons of these countries, thereby diminishing the significance of various past achievements of these movements in the realm of social welfare. Furthermore, people were dying daily, with nothing to show for it except a lingering and corrupting imperialist culture.

At the very same time, in the West, it became increasingly difficult to think of the Communists as a "progressive" alternative to the Social-Democrats, as many had done in the interwar period. For the USSR had become marked with the ineradicable stain of Stalinism and imperial overrule in Eastern Europe. For example, 1956 had been the year of imperialist aggression in Suez. But it had also been the year of Soviet troops in Hungary as well as of Khrushchev's speech. The combination was overwhelming.

Thus, when in 1968, amidst a continuing war in Vietnam, Black Power movements, a growing "counterculture" raging against a consumer society side by side with the "growing gap" between North and South, the rebellious students and workers in the West could turn neither to the Social-Democrats nor to the Communists as ways of expressing their angers and their commitments. Instead, they created a new movement. Its beginnings were so vague that at first it was often called merely "the movement." By the 1970s one began to speak in the plural of the "new social movements."

The shift from the grammatical singular to the plural provides a crucial clue to the nature of the process. For the "movement," if it was ever organizationally singular, soon became multiple, if not necessarily fractionated. That is to say, there emerged a whole series of movements, each organized around a specific theme or focus—movements of "ethnic minorities" or "immigrants," womens' movements, ecology movements, antiwar movements, gay and lesbian movements, movements of the handicapped and of the aged (or pensioners). To be sure, there had been movements of each of these varieties before, sometimes for more than a century. But these movements took on now a different character. Their militance was now directed as much against the hegemony of a Social-Democratic "labor" movement as against anything else. And they were not, despite their formal organizing around a single focus, in fact single-issue organizations. They all seemed to accept, if at first unclearly in many cases, that they formed a part of a larger if amorphous "new social movement," within which their function was to press the interests of one group in a campaign that pressed the common protests of many groups. In short, from the very beginning, the plurality of new social movements implied an obligation felt by each to the mutual solidarity of the multiple new social movements. This principle of mutual solidarity was reflected in the concept, first in the United States, then in France, of a "rainbow coalition."

The situation in the socialist East was quite different. These countries had political systems in which autonomous opposition organizations were quite simply illegal. The "rebellions" had to take a different organizational form than in the West. Secondly, in all these countries, Marxism (indeed Marxism-Leninism) was the official state ideology. Thus while new social movements in the West could be at least *marxisant* (while neither Social-Democratic nor Communist), in the East it was more difficult to use Marxism as an antisystemic language.

The key theme of the new movements in the West was the forgotten people—the ethnic underclasses, the women, the gays, the aged, et cetera. The key theme of the new movements in the East was the newly privileged people—the bureaucrats of the *Nomenklatura*, the party cadres, the police, et cetera. The first signs of a "thaw" were the attempts at mild reform from on top. Khrushchev symbolized such attempts. But those on top soon discovered that it was hard to let the genie out of the bottle in a controlled way. The situation was explosive and the temptation to try to shut the bottle quickly was great.

The story of the anti-"bureaucratic" struggles of the East has been the search, thus far unsuccessful, for a viable organizational form. If we leave out the attempts at anticipatory and cooptative reforms from on top, such as those by Khrushchev or Wladislaw Gomulka in Poland, there have been four quite different major attempts at changing the situation. The first was in Hungary in 1956. There, a top-down anticipatory reformism quickly gave way to a popular upsurge which seemed to be headed in the direction of a multiparty system and the possible detachment of the country from the Eastern bloc. It was suppressed. The second was the Chinese Cultural Revolution, which began in 1966 and went on for a decade. The organizational form was a structured intra-party struggle of "socialist roaders" against "capitalist roaders." Initially, it was politically successful. Eventually, it created its "reign of terror" and had its Thermidor. The third was the attempt to create a "communism with a human face" in Czechoslovakia in 1968, where the new top leadership of the Communist Party would itself take the lead in being antisystemic, in a sense against itself (as well as against Soviet dominance of the Czechoslovak scene). Whether this would have been a viable formula for very long we will never know, since once again the attempt was suppressed by Soviet troops. The fourth form was that adopted in Poland in 1980, the creation of an independent trade union, *Solidarnosc*—independent, that is, both of Communist Party (governmental) control and of any aspiration to state power. *Solidarnosc* represented reform from the bottom up. This form may have been the most viable to date since, despite its legal suppression in 1983, *Solidarnosc* still in fact survives as an antisystemic movement, albeit a weakened one. The fifth form is Gorbachevism, a renewed and more sophisticated Khrushchevism. It promises to be the most long-lasting. Whether it will be in the end permit a stable "public" politics to become institutionalized remains to be demonstrated.

In the third world, the issue has been neither the fact that Social-Democratic reforms forgot half the people nor the fact that Communist reforms created at least as many privileged persons as they removed. It was rather the question that the nationalist and national liberation movements, when all was said and done, were movements that involved cultural assimilation to Western "universalist" practices. Had the "assimilationism" paid off, it might have been acceptable. But after the "independences" and/or the "revolutions," the continuing miserable (often worsening) economic conditions, the frequent neocolonial political subordination, the emergence of new privileged strata even as old privileged strata seemed untouched, all led to a questioning of the premises of even the more "radical" of the historic movements.

What new movements have come along to challenge the older "nationalist" movements? Thus far, many seem to have taken a religious form—the multiple "fundamentalisms" or "integrist" versions not merely of Islam but of Buddhism, Hinduism, Judaism, Christianity. Their politics have been profoundly ambiguous. Liberation theology in Latin America seems openly antisystemic. Khomeinism, in Iran and elsewhere, seems to swing wildly between antisystemic themes and explicitly reactionary ones. The religious form may pass, as the Cultural Revolution form has passed—undermined by its internal contradictions. There has also been a new flourishing of community-level movements, for example in Brazil and India. The search for new forms of antisystemic movement in the third world, organized at least in part around the assertion of the nonacceptability of Western "universalism" (even in its Marxist variant), seems sure to be pursued.

In a very short space of time then, essentially since the 1960s, where previously we had three main varieties of antisystemic movements in the world-system—Social-Democrats largely in the West, Communists largely in the East, and nationalists largely in the third world—we suddenly had six varieties. In addition to the "old" three, we now have the "new social movements" largely in the West, the "antibureaucratic" movements largely in the East, and the "anti-Westernizing" movements largely in the South.

There are two things to notice about this network of six varieties of antisystemic movements. First, each of the six varieties is specifically critical of the other five. Secondly, there are some themes common to the older three varieties and some themes common to the newer three varieties.

We have already reviewed the criticism of each of the three new varieties of that old variety that is located in its own zone. And we are quite aware of the ripostes of each of the old varieties to that new one in its own zone. The Social-Democrats have tended to argue of the new social movements that they are unreasonable in their demands and thereby threaten the security of the gains in social welfare acquired by 100 years of past struggle. The Communists have tended to argue of the antibureaucratic movements that they undermine the stability of the state and of the worldwide antisystemic struggle. The nationalist movements have tended to argue of the "anti-Westernizing" movements that they undermine the possibilities of economic transformation and move in fact in the direction of social stagnation.

These mutual criticisms are not the end of the story. Each "new" variety of movement tends to be critical as well of each other "new" variety on the grounds that its demands are parochial (that is, in the context of the worldsystem, primarily concerned with its "zone"). And each "new" variety of movement tends to be critical of the two "old" varieties outside its "zone" on the grounds that they are not truly antisystemic, and are concerned more with coming to terms with the groups in power in their "zone" than with supporting (or even approving of) the "new" antisystemic thrusts. And finally, each "old" variety is critical not only of each other "old" variety (for reasons already reviewed) but of the "new" varieties outside its zone, on the grounds that they have not embraced its particular variant of "old" variety as the mode of struggle against that "old" variety which the "new" movement is primarily criticizing. In short, with six varieties extant, we seem to have a war of all against all, and one in which all sides seem to have very telling arguments against the other five.

Nonetheless, as we have said, there are some common themes of the "old" varieties versus the "new" varieties. We have reviewed the fact that each of the "old" varieties accepts a common strategic premise—that in the middle run, there must be a two-stage political process: first, political mobilization to achieve state power; then, political consolidation to transform the "national society." It is precisely the activities based on this strategic premise which have brought about not only the very real political reforms of the twentieth century (particularly after 1945) but also the various impasses we have detailed.

Consequently, what unites all three "new" varieties is their profound skepticism of these premises, in many cases their explicit rejection of the legitimacy and utility of the strategy. To the refrain of the "old" movements—our present problems will disappear when our traditional strategy is carried out in still more countries—the "new" movements have shouted "enough!" Let us not throw good money after bad. The strategy of the "old" movements has failed. It has not changed the world. Let us find a new strategy. The major problem is that the "new" varieties of movements have not been very clear on what alternative strategy they have to offer.

This is precisely the "crisis" of the movements, taken collectively. The "old" movements have pursued with considerable success a strategy. They have attained state power in many, many countries. We now have the experience of their "success" behind us. The "successes" have had sufficiently ambiguous results that three new whole varieties of movements have come into existence precisely to contest the old strategy. But the new varieties have yet to make clear a viable alternative strategy and therefore have been unable to mobilize support systematically and consistently.

Is there a plausible way in which this "crisis of the movements" can be resolved? Let us start by noting one very positive factor in the situation. In the immediate postwar period, the three "old" varieties had reached a stage of quite shrill mutual denunciations and suspicions. In the 1960s, the emergent "new" varieties raised the decibel level even higher. There came a point at which it seemed that all was internecine warfare among the antisystemic movements.

But 1968 and its sequels had its cathartic side as well. On the one hand, the harsh criticisms by the "new" movements of the "old" ones finally seemed to break the rigid ideological crust of dogmatic self-confidence that the old movements exhibited. In that way, the 1960s opened the space for reflection and rethinking. On the other hand, the failures of the early efforts of the new movements became quite visible after a few years. This in turn squashed the incipient dogmatisms of the new movements. In that way, the 1970s preserved the space for reflection and rethinking.

What we have seen lately, in the 1980s, is a series of tentative steps by the six varieties of movements to talk to each other, to talk to all of the others. It is not that the traditional suspicions have been eradicated. It is rather that the arrogances have been toned down, and the common heritage remembered. What common heritage, you may ask? The common heritage is that, when all is said and done, all these movements (as movements) emerged out of a rejection of the injustices of the existing world-system, the capitalist world-economy. Each in its own way was seeking to fulfill the slogan of the French Revolution: more liberty, more equality, more fraternity.

No doubt there has been much cooptation and no doubt there has been too often a too narrow definition of who should benefit from the drive for liberty, equality, and fraternity. But these movements have had the degree of success they have had only because of popular support. And for the most part this popular support has been given because these movements were seen as antisystemic. To the extent that they were not, they have lost legitimacy and bred their own oppositions.

It seems clear in which direction we must head. On the one hand, we must head in the direction of creating a family of antisystemic movements that will have a place in it for all six "varieties" that have come to be constituted—a grand coalition that can not be based on any strong centralization that implies the hegemony of any one variety. On the other hand, we must worry about the fact that each of the six varieties contains within it important elements that are no longer antisystemic in spirit. These elements have to go. But if they are "purged," we shall immediately be back onto the road of organizational dogmatism that has been in large part responsible for the present impasse. These elements that are not antisystemic will however leave of their own accord if and when these movements—or the family of movements—reaffirm in concrete operational ways their commitment to transforming the capitalist world-economy into a world order that will be libertarian, egalitarian, fraternal.

The family of movements therefore has two immediate tasks, that is, tasks of the next twenty years. It must begin to think more concretely about the long-range objective, of what it means in institutional terms to create a world order that is libertarian, egalitarian, fraternal. An exercise in Utopia, you say? Perhaps, but a bit more clarity about our utopia could serve the function both of knitting together the family of movements (overcoming the mutual suspicions) and forcing out the elements that are not ready to be antisystemic.

The second immediate task is to rethink the intermediate stategy. This will not be easy. There is nothing inevitable about the achievement of our long-run goals. Even if it can be demonstrated that the present historical system is doomed by its contradictions (and I believe this can in fact be demonstrated) it does not follow that the successor system or systems will necessarily be better. It may follow, but it does not have to follow. Whether it does will be a collective social decision, and there will be, there is, a real struggle about this decision. It is the choice of intermediate strategy by the movements that will largely determine in which direction the systemic transition will go.

The question is of course a political one. If in the nineteenth century our predecessors concluded that the correct option was to seek to attain state power, it was because the state loomed so large as a locus of real power. This was not an incorrect perception. The state, the controller of "legitimate violence" (as Weber put it), loomed large then and looms even larger now. Its role has not receded.

And yet, of course, we have also learned in these last 100 years that the state has less power than it seems to have. One revolutionary government after another has discovered the limitations of state power, has discovered all the things it could not do even when it seemed to have this so-called monopoly of legitimate violence. The limitations have been felt in two ways. There have been the restraints from "without"—the overt politico-military pressures of other states, the indirect but very real pressures that transcended political boundaries. And there have been the restraints from "within"—the fact that the cadres of any regime were persons with interests (personal interests, collective interests) and pursued them willy-nilly in terms of the logic and the possibilities of the world-system of which they are a part; the fact that even if one abolishes political factions within a state, different (class) interests could always find a way to express themselves and to impose themselves on state policy.

If obtaining state power is something but scarcely everything, what alternative objectives can movements give themselves over the middle run? One possibility is to start by taking cognizance of the fact that, although the state is a major locus of power, it is not the only locus of power in our current historical system. Control of economic resources is clearly a way of having power. And, as Gramsci regularly reminded us, so is control of the intellectual definition of the situation. There are also all the non-state institutional structures—the cultural institutions, the press, the schools, the health institutions, the syndicates, the voluntary associations. Each has some power. Furthermore, of course, there is local power as well as statewide power.

Once we recognize that in practice power is enormously diffuse, we can see that the conquest of power by the family of antisystemic movements involves far more than the conquest of state power, which, if not secondary in importance, may at least be secondary in temporal sequence. Whatever strategy we construct must give up this blind faith that controlling the state apparatus is the key to everything else; it may well be that everything else is the key to controlling the state apparatus.

In any case, our strategy must be truly global. All of the nineteenth-century movements gave lip service to international solidarity. But in practice politics has been primarily, virtually exclusively, national. The construction of a world politics, one actually practiced by antisystemic movements, is still for the future. The new strategy must implement such a world politics.

What is happening is a dialogue among the movements. It is not at all unreasonable to believe that this dialogue can in fact result in a new consensus on strategy. It is not a question of a "fresh start." It is rather a question of the critical analysis of past experience and present failures, of seeking to preserve what has been gained from struggles of the 1850–1950 period (both the concrete institutions and the intellectual understanding) and add to it a strong dash of daring new approaches derived from the post-1945 experience. The combination might work.

4. Agenda for the Movements

The lesson of 1848 was that spontaneous uprisings were not viable as a path of serious social or national revolution. Social transformation required social organization. It was out of this lesson that the "old" antisystemic movements were born. We have argued that 1968 marked the emergence of "new" antisystemic movements that were protesting against the successes (that we see as failures) of the "old" antisystemic movements.

The lesson of 1968 has been that it is not so easy to find a practical organizational substitute for the strategy of the "old" antisystemic movements. The euphoria of 1968 lasted a few years but has been followed by confusion, uncertainty, sometimes disarray. This has not been entirely negative, as we have noted, since the total experience has at least permitted the reopening of the intellectual debate within and among the movements. What therefore follows in terms of concrete political action in the relatively short run?

1. The first objective must be the repoliticization of the mass base (and indeed of the cadres) of the movements. One of the major results of the "1968" onslaught of the new movements against the old movements, followed by the subsequent exhaustion of so many of the organizations spawned by the new movements in the 1970s, has been a widespread lassitude. There has been much organizational disillusionment, and large numbers of persons have withdrawn from party structures and even from non-party organizations. While there has always been a pattern of cyclical

ups and downs of organizational involvement, the skepticism about organizations seems deeper now, precisely because of the "crisis of the movements."

The ball is in the court of the movements. What is no doubt required is that movements rethink their internal organizational patterns. The quasimilitary, hierarchical structures of the old movements—a structure that evolved because they were seeking state power—was precisely one of the things to which the new movements had objected, only to replicate the patterns themselves as the 1970s proceeded. On the other hand, the total antileadership bias of some of the new movements (such as the German Greens, at least in the beginning) seems a recipe for inefficacy and, therefore, of disillusionment and depoliticization in the long run as well.

The problem is the invention of new forms of movement participation that will founder neither on the shoals of a mythically "democratic" centralism nor on a plebisicitarian antipathy to leadership itself. This is not a problem that can be tackled merely at the level of formal organizational structure. It is closely linked to the question of real program. A movement that seeks to achieve social transformation by seeking to persuade and to change at *every* level of the world-system, from the very local arenas to the functional institutional arenas to the state structures to the realms of culture and knowledge requires and will have to contruct new and more imaginative organizational forms, ones that allow more space for internal discussion, that operate in longer time spans, that assume more mature members.

It is a circular process. No effective social transformation can be obtained without some significant repoliticization. No significant political involvement will be achieved without organizational restructuring. But the restructuring itself will be in part a function of an ongoing social transformation.

2. Thus there is a second urgent object—the reconceptualization of our understanding of the process of social transformation itself. The "old" movements were born in the nineteenth-century world. They very naturally based themselves on a nineteenth-century view of the world. The social turmoil that ran approximately from 1763 to 1848, and which is incarnated most strikingly in the French Revolution, revolved around a few central themes. One was the acceptance of the Enlightenment perspective of the inevitability of progress. The second was the new importance given to three phenomena which were not absolutely new, but had never before been considered politically central: the dynamics of industrial

production, the self-assertion of the bourgeoisie, and the sense of the nation as the incarnation of a "people," a people which now was asserting its "sovereignty."

This set of political developments—in fact, we should call it a set of political options—led to a mode of theorizing about the social world congruent with the needs of the new political forces. The theorizing was centered around the assumption that each sovereign state—or at least those built around "historical nations," to remember Marx's infelicitous phrase—reflected separately a universal pattern of social transformation reflecting a technological evolution. It was further believe that the stages of such transformation were punctured by a series of dramatic transitions, or "revolutions," and that, in the capitalist world, the essential struggle had been the coming to power of a bourgeoisie in rebellion against an aristocracy.

It is not necessary here to spell out the complex elaborations to which these simple premises led, or to show in detail how the three historical varieties of "old" movements utilized, each in its own way, these premises to determine not only their middle-run strategies but even their short-run tactics. Nor is it necessary here to show how their practical policies intermeshed with the more abstract theorizing that characterized the newly emerging so-called disciplines of history and the various social sciences.

It is enough to remember that the nineteenth-century theorizing of the movements led to predictions that have been dramatically falsified by history. There have been three main expectations of the nineteenth-century movements which, seen from the perspective of the late twentieth century, have turned out to be not correct.

The first was the expectation that there was operating what might be called a vector of world-level homogenization. It was theorized that, since over time, all states reflected a singular evolutionary process, over time the different parts of the world would look increasingly the same. This assumption has turned out to be dramatically wrong. World-wide polarization (in terms not merely of wealth but of structure) has instead been the central reality. By the 1960s, the theoretical expectation of world-level homogenization was being challenged by an alternative expectation of the "development of underdevelopment," in Frank's famous phrase.

The second expectation was the isomorphic one of homogenization at the level of each individual state. This expectation was that over time the various particularisms of race, religion, ethnicity, and so on would disappear or be "overcome" as atavistic survivals of a premodern world, all subsumed in single peoplehoods, guaranteed by the legal concept of citizenship. If peoples were divided at all, it was only on the "objective" class grounds, and this too would eventually be overcome by a final social transformation. Once again, historical reality has turned out to be dramatically different. The "particularisms" have if anything increased in social importance. Racism, in its manifold variants, has come to be seen as a central reality in all states. And sexism has come to be understood as a parallel social reality, whose significance has *not* been decreasing. Thus, again by the 1960s, the theoretical expectation that class was the only significant organizing basis of national stratification was being widely challenged by the insistence that race/ethnicity and gender were equally, if not more, important.

The third expectation was that, as the economic situation of the world "deteriorated," oppressed groups throughout the world would be increasingly willing to assert their rights militantly and to engage in insurrectionary activities. This has turned out to be a very partial truth at best. No doubt there has been much militance and a considerable amount of insurrectionary activity over the past 150 years. But the vector has certainly not been a positive linear one. Whether at a state-level or at the world-level, the vector has been, if not cyclical, then curvilinear. It is certainly not at all clear today that we can anticipate a significant increase in insurrectionary activities in the decades to come.

Thus, nineteenth-century theorizing, recounted here in terms of the historical expectations to which it led and which inspired the strategy of the antisystemic movements, has turned out to have been seriously in error in some fundamental ways. It follows that if antisystemic movements are to achieve significant results in the decades to come, they will have to participate in a process of fundamental reconceptualization of our underlying social theory. This is not a small task nor one that can be done swiftly. The process of reconceptualizing has already begun. Indeed the "new" antisystemic movements were themselves the catalyst of a good deal of this. But it is a task that has yet to be completed and still needs a great deal of collective energy to complete.

3. The third objective is the bringing together of the six varieties of antisystemic movements into a worldwide "family" of movements. The analogy of a."family" is deliberate. Families do not always agree. And adult siblings move on their separate roads, each along lines he or she thinks best. But families are presumed to share some history, some values, and to

manifest some community, especially when they have to face hostile outsiders.

In practical terms, this means several things on the part of existing movements. It means first of all a conscious effort at empathetic understanding of the other movements, their histories, their priorities, their social bases, their current concerns. Correspondingly, increased empathy needs to be accompanied by restraint in rhetoric. It does not mean that movements should not be frank with each other, even in public. It means that the discussion needs to be self-consciously comradely, based on the recognition of a unifying objective, a relatively democratic, relatively egalitarian world.

Consequently, this means that the movements will have to devote considerably more energy than has historically been the case to intermovement diplomacy. To the extent that the movements come to internalize the sense that the social transformation they are seeking will not occur in a single apocalyptic moment, but as a continuous process, one continually hard-fought, they may learn to concentrate their energies somewhat less exclusively on the immediate tactics of change and somewhat more on constructing middle-run stepping-stones. In such a context, intramovement diplomacy becomes a very useful expenditure of energy. It will make possible the combination of daring leaps and structural consolidation which could make plausible a progressive transformation of the world-system.

4. Finally, the fourth objective must be the deghettoization of the antisystemic movements. Now more than ever we have a multiplicity of antisystemic movements around the globe. Each has its particular social base, and each builds its strength by reinforcing the social consciousness of its base group, and hence in a sense its sense of "separatism." No doubt this has been and will remain a key element in the politicization of the oppressed. For the only place to start in political organizing is where people find themselves. That is, one can only organize people politically around issues that are meaningful to them in their ordinary, ongoing social lives.

"Separatism" in this sense is an indispensable mode of becoming self-aware socially, that is, of fully understanding the real oppressive structures of the world-system. But "separatism" is only a stepping-stone, never a solution.

Not only can no particular "separated" group obtain its objectives separately, but of course in the long run the opposite is true. Antisystemic transformation requires alliances, is only possible under the condition of middle-run alliances. Of course, all movements have always been ready to engage in short-run tactical alliances. But middle-run strategic ones are a different story. This is the obverse face of intramovement diplomacy. This is what intramovement diplomacy is all about.

In the process of deghettoization, it is important to remember that it is not the case that *some* movements are "universalistic" and *others* "particularistic." *All* existing movements are in some ghetto. Each must get out of its ghetto in order to construct the "family" of movements, the alliance of the multiple groups of the oppressed.

5. It may seem that I have preached the very obvious: the need for repoliticization, reconceptualization, construction of a "family" of movements, deghettoization. And yet a moment's reflection will remind us that, if these are obvious verities, they are not yet practiced by a large number of the world's antisystemic movements. And there are indeed many obstacles to the widespread adoption of these objectives.

It is only however, in my view, when (and if) such objectives will become widely accepted that we can seriously begin to believe that the eventual decline of the world capitalist system may in fact lead to the construction of a world order that would be both relatively democratic and relatively egalitarian.

MARXIST CENTURY—AMERICAN CENTURY: THE MAKING AND REMAKING OF THE WORLD LABOR MOVEMENT

Giovanni Arrighi

1. *The Communist Manifesto Revisited*

In the closing paragraphs of the first section of *The Communist Manifesto*, Marx and Engels make two predictions about the future of bourgeois society that seem to contradict each other. On the one hand, they predict that the rule of the bourgeoisie will come to an end because it lets the proletariat sink deeper and deeper into pauperism:

> [The bourgeoisie] is unfit to rule because it is incompetent to assure an existence to its slave within its slavery, because it cannot help letting him sink into such a state, that it has to feed him, instead of being fed by him. Society cannot live under this bourgeoisie, in other words, its existence is no longer compatible with society. (1967: 93)

On the other hand, they predict that the rule of the bourgeoisie will come to an end because, unwittingly but inevitably, it undermines the essential condition of its own existence, competition among the laborers:

> The advance of industry, whose involuntary promoter is the bourgeoisie, replaces the isolation of the labourers, due to competition, by their revolutionary combination, due to association. The development of Modern Industry, therefore, cuts from under its feet the very foundation on which the bourgeoisie produces and appropriates products. What the bourgeoisie, therefore, produces, above all, is its own grave diggers. Its fall and the victory of the proletariat are equally inevitable. (1967: 93–94)

The thesis here is that these two predictions represent both the strength and the weakness of the Marxian legacy. They represent its strength because they have been validated in many crucial respects by fundamental trends of the capitalist world-economy in the subsequent 140 years. And they represent its weakness because the two scenarios are in partial contradiction with each other and, what's more, the contradiction has lived on unresolved in the theories and practices of Marx's followers.

The contradiction, as I see it, is the following. The first scenario is of proletarian helplessness. Competition prevents the proletariat from sharing the benefits of industrial progress, and drives it into such a state of poverty that, instead of a productive force, it becomes a dead weight on society. The second scenario, in contrast, is of proletarian power. The advance of industry replaces competition with association among proletarians so that the ability of the bourgeoisie to appropriate the benefits of industrial progress is undermined.

For Marx, of course, there was no contradiction between these two scenarios. The tendency toward the weakening of the proletariat concerned the Industrial Reserve Army and undermined the *legitimacy* of bourgeois rule. The tendency toward the strengthening of the proletariat concerned the Active Industrial Army and undermined the capacity of the bourgeoisie to appropriate surplus.

Moreover, these two tendencies were not conceived as being independent of one another. To the extent that the capacity of the bourgeosie to appropriate surplus is undermined, two effects concerning the Industrial Reserve Army follow. The means available to the bourgeoisie to "feed," that is, to reproduce the Reserve Army are reduced, while the incentive to employ proletarian labor as a means to augment capital also decreases and, *ceteris paribus*, the Reserve Army increases. Hence, any increase in the power of the Active Industrial Army to resist exploitation is translated more or less automatically in a loss of legitimacy of the bourgeois order.

At the same time, any loss of legitimacy of bourgeois rule due to its inability to assure the livelihood of the Reserve Army is translated more or less automatically into a greater (and qualitatively superior) power of the Active Army. For in Marx's view the Active and the Reserve armies consisted of the same human material which was assumed to circulate more or less continuously from the one to the other. The same individuals would be part of the Active Army today and of the Reserve Army tomorrow, depending on the continuous ups and downs of enterprises, lines and locales of production. The bourgeois order would thus lose legitimacy among the members of the Reserve and Active armies alike, thereby enhancing the tendency of whomever happens to be in the Active Army to turn their association in the productive process from an instrument of exploitation by the bourgeoisie into an instrument of struggle against the bourgeoisie.

The power of this model lies in its simplicity. It is based on three postulates. First, as Marx was to state in Volume 3 of *Capital*, the limit of capital is capital itself. That is to say, the evolution and the eventual demise of capital are written in its "genes." The dynamic element in the evolution and eventual demise of capital is "the advancement of industry." Capitalist accumulation can proceed only if it advances industry, but the advancement of industry replaces competition among the workers, on which accumulation rests, with their association. Sooner or later, capitalist accumulation becomes self-defeating.

This deterministic view of the processes of capitalist accumulation, however, applies only to the system as a whole and over long periods of time. The outcome of the process at particular places and at particular times is left entirely indeterminate by the model. There are defeats and victories of the proletariat but both are necessarily temporary and localized events. The logic of competition among capitalist enterprises and among proletarians has an "averaging effect" on defeats and victories. The only thing that is inevitable in the model is that in the very long run capitalist accumulation creates the conditions for an increase in the number of proletarian victories over proletarian defeats until bourgeois rule is displaced, replaced, or transformed beyond recognition.

The time and modalities of the transition to a post-bourgeois order are also left indeterminate. Precisely because the transition was made to depend on a multiplicity of victories and defeats combined spatially and temporally in unpredictable ways, little was said in the *Manifesto* about the contours of the future society, except that it would bear the imprints of proletarian culture—whatever that culture would be at the time of the transition.

A second postulate is that the subjects of long-term, large-scale social change are personifications of structural tendencies. Competition among individual members of the bourgeoisie ensures the advancement of industry, while competition among the individual members of the proletariat ensures that the benefits of the advancement accrue to the bourgeoisie. But the advancement of industry means an ever-widening cooperation within and among labor processes. At a certain stage of development, this ever-widening cooperation transforms the proletariat from an ensemble of competing individuals into a cohesive class capable of putting an end to exploitation.

Consciousness and organization are reflections of structural processes of competition and cooperation which are not due to any individual or collective will. The multiple struggles waged by proletarians are an essential ingredient in the transformation of structural change into ideological and organizational change, but are themselves rooted in structural changes. This is the only "understanding" that can be usefully "brought to" the proletariat from outside its condition:

> The Communists do not form a separate party opposed to other working-class parties.
>
> They have no interests separate and apart from those of the proletariat as a whole.
>
> They do not set up any sectarian principles of their own, by which to shape and mould the proletarian movement.
>
> The Communists are distinguished from the other working-class parties by this only: 1. In the national struggles of the proletarians of the different countries, they point out and bring to the front the common interests of the entire proletariat, independently of all nationality. 2. In the various stages of development which the struggles of the working class against the bourgeoisie has to pass through, they always and everywhere represent the interests of the movement as a whole. (Marx and Engels 1967: 95)

The third postulate of the model is the primacy of the economy over culture and politics. The proletariat itself is defined in purely economic terms as "a class of labourers, who live only as long as they find work, and who find work only so long as their labour increases capital. These labourers, who must sell themselves piecemeal, are a commodity, like every article of commerce, and are consequently exposed to all the vicissitudes of competition, to all the fluctuations of the market" (1967: 87).[1]

To be sure, the entire work of Marx was aimed at disclosing the fiction involved in treating labor as a commodity like any other. Being inseparable from its owner, and hence endowed with a will and an intelligence, the commodity labor power was different from all other "articles of commerce." Yet, in the Marxian scheme this fictitious character of the commodity labor power appears only in the struggles of the proletariat against the bourgeoisie, and even there only as an undifferentiated proletarian will and intelligence. Individual and group differences within the proletariat are minimized or dismissed as residuals of the past in the process of being eliminated by the laws of market competition. The proletarian has neither country nor family:

> Differences of age and sex have no longer any distinctive social validity for the working class. All are instruments of labor, more or less expensive to use, according to their age and sex. (1967: 88)

[Modern] subjection to capital, the same in England as in France, in America as in Germany, has stripped him of every trace of national character. . . . National differences and antagonisms between peoples are daily more and more vanishing, owing to the development of the bourgeoisie, to freedom of commerce, to the world market, to uniformity in the mode of production and in the conditions of life corresponding thereto. (1967: 92, 102)

In the Marxian scheme, therefore, the proletarian is either an atomized individual competing with other (equally atomized) individuals over the means of subsistence, or a member of a universal class struggling against the bourgeoisie. Between the universal class and the atomized individual there is no intermediate aggregation capable of supplying security or status in competition with class membership. Market competition makes all such intermediate aggregations unstable and, hence, transient.

Similarly, the Marxian scheme reduces power struggles to a mere reflection of market competition or of the class struggle. There is no room for the pursuit of power for its own sake. The only thing that is pursued for its own sake is profit, the principal form of surplus through which historical accumulation takes place. Governments are instruments of competition or class rule, simple committees "for managing the common affairs of the whole bourgeoisie." Once again, it is market competition that forces governments into this mold. If they do not conform to the rules of the capitalist game, they are bound to lose out also in the power game:

> The cheap prices of [its] commodities are the heavy artillery with which [the bourgeoisie] batters down all Chinese walls, with which it forces the barbarians' intensely obstinate hatred of foreigners to capitulate. It compels all nations, on pain of extinction, to adopt the bourgeois mode of production; it compels them to introduce what it calls civilization into their midst, i.e., to become bourgeois themselves. In one word, it creates a world after its own image. (1967: 84)

In sum, the Marxian legacy consisted originally of a model of bourgeois society which made three strong predictions:

(1) Bourgeois society tends to polarize into two classes, the bourgeoisie itself and the proletariat, understood as a class of workers who live only so long as they find work, and who find work only so long as their labor increases capital.

(2) Capitalist accumulation tends to impoverish and, simultaneously, to strengthen the proletariat within bourgeois society. The strengthening relates to the role of the proletariat as producer of social wealth, the impoverishment relates to its role as more or less commodified labor power subject to all the vicissitudes of competition.

(3) The socially—and politically—blind laws of market competition tend to merge these two tendencies into a general loss of legitimacy of the bourgeois order which provokes its supersession by a noncompetitive, nonexploitative world order.

In order to assess the extent to which these predictions have been borne out by the subsequent history of capitalism, it is useful to break up the 140 years that separate us from 1848 into three periods of roughly equal length: 1848 to 1896; 1896 to 1948; and 1948 to the present. This periodization is meaningful for many of the problems at hand. The periods all correspond to a "long wave" of economic activity, each comprising a phase of "prosperity," in which relations of cooperation in the economy are predominant (A phases), and a phase of "depression," in which relations of competition predominate (B phases). Besides that, each fifty-year period has its own specificities.

Between 1848 and 1896 market capitalism and bourgeois society, as analyzed by Marx, reached their apogee. The modern labor movement was born in this period and immediately became the central antisystemic force. After a protracted struggle against rival doctrines, Marxism became the dominant ideology of the movement. In the period 1896 to 1948 market capitalism and bourgeois society as theorized by Marx entered a prolonged and ultimately fatal crisis. The labor movement reached its apogee as the central antisystemic force, and Marxism consolidated and extended its hegemony over antisystemic movements. However, new divisions appeared within and among antisystemic movements, and Marxism itself was split apart, into a revolutionary and a reformist wing. After 1948 corporate or managerial capitalism emerged from the ashes of market capitalism as the dominant world-economic structure. The spread of antisystemic movements increased further but so did their fragmentation and reciprocal antagonisms. Under the pressure of these antagonisms, Marxism has been thrown into a crisis from which it has yet to recover and, indeed, may never recover.

2. The Rise of the World Labor Movement

The major trends and events of the first period (1848–96) conform to the expectations of the *Manifesto*. The spread of free-trade practices and the transport revolution in the twenty or twenty-five years that followed 1848 made market capitalism more of a worldwide reality than it had ever been before. World-market competition intensified and industry expanded rapidly for most of the fifty-year period.

The proletarianization of intermediate strata became more widespread, though not as widespread and irreversible as it is often claimed. Partly because of the contraction of the intermediate strata, partly because of a widening gap between the incomes of proletarian and bourgeois households, and partly because of the greater residential concentration and segregation of the proletariat, the polarization of society into two distinct and counterposed classes seemed an indisputable tendency, though more so in some countries than in others.

The tendency of capitalist accumulation to simultaneously impoverish and strengthen the proletariat was also in evidence. The greater concentration of the proletariat associated with the spread of industrialization made its organization in the form of unions much easier, and the strategic position of wage workers in the new production processes endowed these organizations with considerable power, not only vis-à-vis capitalist employers, but vis-à-vis governments as well. The successes of the British labor movement in the course of the mid-nineteenth-century A phase in limiting the length of the working day and in extending the franchise were the most visible but not the only expression of such power.

Yet, the proletariat was also being impoverished. Each victory had to be sanctioned by market forces, which narrowly constrained the capacity of workers to resist the economic and political command of the bourgeoisie. It is in this period that unemployment acquired qualitatively and quantitatively new dimensions that curtailed the improvements in the proletariat's working and living conditions and intensified competitive pressures in its midst.

Finally, as predicted by the *Manifesto*, the two opposing tendencies of impoverishment and strengthening jointly undermined proletarian consent for bourgeois rule. A relatively free circulation of commodities, capital, and workers within and across state jurisdictions spread the costs and risks of unemployment among proletarian households. The consequent loss of legitimacy led to an entirely new degree of political autonomy of the proletariat from the bourgeoisie. The era of working-class political parties only begins in this period. But whether or not working-class parties had come into existence, wage workers in all core countries shook off their traditional subordination to the political interests of the bourgeoisie and began to pursue their own interests autonomously from, and if necessary against, the bourgeoisie.

The most spectacular (and dramatic) expression of this political emancipation of the proletariat was the Paris Commune of 1871. In the Paris

Commune, the proletariat for the first time held political power "for two whole months" (as Marx and Engels wrote enthusiastically in the preface to the 1872 German edition of the *Manifesto*). Although defeated, the Paris Commune was hailed by Marx as exemplary of the future organization of the proletariat as the ruling class.

The close fit of the trends and events of 1848–96 with the predictions of the *Manifesto* goes a long way toward explaining the success of Marx and his followers in establishing their hegemony over the nascent European labor movement. Their success came only after protracted intellectual struggles over whether proletarianization was historically irreversible—and so formed the proper ground on which to carry forward the struggles of the present for the society of the future as theorized by Marx—or whether proletarians could historically recover their lost economic independence through one form or another of cooperative production. The latter view had been propounded in earlier periods by the Owenites in England and the Fourierists in France but lived on in new and different forms among the followers of Proudhon and Bakunin in France, Belgium, Russia, Italy, and Spain and of Lassalle in Germany.

The First International was little more than a sounding board of this intellectual struggle, which saw Marx on the side of British trade unionists (the only real representatives of an actually existing industrial proletariat) against a mixed bag of revolutionary and reformist intellectuals (some of working-class extraction) from Continental Europe. Even though Marx pretty much ran the show, he never won a clear-cut victory and, when he did, the impact on the real movement was illusory. The moment of truth came with the Paris Commune. The conclusions that Marx drew from that experience (the need to constitute legal working-class parties in each country as the presupposition of socialist revolution) alienated, for opposite reasons, Continental revolutionaries and British trade unionists alike, and the end of the International was sealed (cf. Abendroth 1973).

Just as the First International was disintegrating with no winners and many losers around 1873, the mid-nineteenth-century phase of "prosperity" turned into the late-nineteenth-century Great Depression, and the conditions were created both for the labor movement in its modern form to take off and for Marxists to establish hegemony over the movement. Intensifying competitive pressures widened and deepened processes of proletarianization and multiplied the occasions of conflict between labor and capital. Between 1873 and 1896, strike activity on an unprecedented scale developed in one country after the other, while working-class parties were being established throughout Europe along the lines recommended by Marx in 1871. By 1896 a new International, this time based on working-class parties with a broad unity of purpose, had become a reality.

The success of the *Manifesto* in predicting the broad contours of the subsequent fifty years was and is quite impressive. Yet not all the relevant facts fitted into the Marxian scheme. The most important anomaly was proletarian politics itself.

The only major attempt by the proletariat to seize state power and constitute itself as the ruling class along the lines theorized by Marx, the Paris Commune, was almost completely unrelated to the kind of tendencies that according to that theory were supposed to bring about such a revolutionary takeover. It was not the outcome of structural factors (a strengthening of the proletariat, due to the advancement of industry, combined with its growing impoverishment, due to commodification) but mainly the outcome of political factors: the defeat of France by Prussia and the harsh conditions created by the Franco-Prussian war. That is to say, the proletariat attempted a political revolution, not because of a growing contradiction between its increasing exploitation and its increasing power in production processes, but because the bourgeois state had proved to be incompetent in "protecting" French society in general, and the Parisian proletariat in particular, from/against another state.

It may be argued that the defeat in war was only the detonator of structural contradictions which were the real, that is, deeper cause of the explosion. The problem with this objection is that where structural contradictions were most developed (in England, throughout the period under examination, in the United States, from the late 1870s onward) the level of direct class warfare between labor and capital (as gauged, for example, by strike activity) was indeed much higher than elsewhere.[2] Yet, labor unrest in these countries showed no propensity whatsoever to turn into political revolution. If the British industrial proletariat (by far the most developed as a class in itself, and the most prone to strike activity, around 1871) had the slightest propensity toward political revolution, its representatives in the First International would have taken a more positive attitude toward the Paris Commune than they actually did. Their negative attitude was in fact symptomatic of a major problem with the Marxian scheme, and probably played a role in inducing Marx to abandon his active involvement in labor politics.

The disjunction between direct and more roundabout forms of the class struggle was confirmed after the Paris Commune in a different way. As mentioned earlier on, the coming of the late-nineteenth-century Great Depression coincided with a major upsurge in strike activity (the most direct form of class struggle) and the formation of national working-class parties (a roundabout form of class struggle). Even though these two tendencies seemed to validate the predictions of the *Manifesto*, their spatial separation could not be fitted easily into the Marxian scheme. The countries that were leading in strike activity (Britain and the United States) were laggards in the formation of working-class parties, while the leading country in the process of working-class party formation (Germany) was a laggard in strike activity. Generally speaking, the formation of working-class parties seemed to have little to do with economic exploitation, working-class formation, and structural conflict between labor and capital. Rather, the main determinants seemed to be the actual and perceived centrality of the state in social and economic regulation, and the struggle for basic civil rights (rights to assembly and to vote in the first place) of and for the proletariat. In Germany, where the state was highly visible and a growing industrial proletariat was denied basic civil rights, the class struggle took the roundabout form of the organization of a working-class party. It was only at the end of the Great Depression, and above all in the subsequent A phase, that the class struggle took the form of a direct clash between labor and capital. In Britain and the United States, where the state was less centrally organized and the proletariat already had secured basic civil rights, the class struggle took the form of strike activity and trade-union formation, and only much later (in Britain) or never (in the United States) did attempts to form nationally significant working-class parties succeed.

These differences will be further discussed in the next section. For now let us simply notice that the history of the class struggle in the first fifty years after the publication of the *Manifesto* provided both strong evidence in support of its main predictions, *and* some food for thought on the validity of the relationship between class struggle and socialist revolution postulated by Marx and Engels. More specifically, the socioeconomic formation of the industrial proletariat did lead to the development of structural forms of class struggle, but did not lead to the development of political, let alone politically revolutionary, tendencies within the proletariat. The attitude of the proletariat toward political power remained purely instrumental, *unless*, as in Continental Europe, political conditions themselves (relations among states, and relations between states and their subjects) prompted more direct, and if necessary revolutionary, participation in political activity.

In the context of the great advances of the labor movement (and of Marxism within the labor movement) of the late nineteenth century, these anomalies must have looked like details unworthy of much consideration. Moreover, it was still reasonable to expect that the invisible hand of the market would take care of these national discrepancies, and make the labor movement of all countries converge toward a common parttern of struggle, consciousness, and organization. As it turned out, what had been a minor anomaly in the late nineteenth century became in the next half century a major historical trend which split the labor movement into two opposite and antagonistic camps.

3. *Global Wars, Movements, and Revolution*

Between 1896 and 1948 the orderliness of world-market rule for political and social actors broke down, and Marx's expectation of an increasing homogenization of the conditions of existence of the world proletariat went unfulfilled. Following nineteenth-century liberal ideology, Marx had assumed that the world market operated over the heads rather than through the hands of state actors. This turned out to be a major misconception because the world market of his time was first and foremost an instrument of British rule over the expanded European state system. As such, its effectiveness rested on a particular distribution of power and wealth among a multiplicity of ruling groups whose continuing consent, or at least acquiescence, was essential to the continuation of British hegemony.

The Great Depression of 1873–96 was both the high and the terminal point of world-market rule as instituted in the nineteenth century. A major aspect of the depression was the arrival in Europe of massive and cheap overseas (and Russian) grain supplies. The main beneficiaries of this inflow were the overseas suppliers (the United States in the first place) and the hegemonic power itself, which was the main importer of overseas grain and controlled most of world commercial and financial intermediation. The main loser was Germany, whose rapidly rising wealth and power still relied heavily on the domestic production of grain and very little on the organization of world commerce and finance. Threatened by this development, the German ruling classes responded to the challenge through a further build-up of their military-industrial complex in an attempt to displace or join Britain at the commanding heights of the world-economy.

The result was a generalized and open power struggle in the interstate system which took world wars to resolve.

In the course of this struggle, world-market rule was impaired and, during and after World War I, suspended. The demise of world-market rule did not stop the "advancement of industry" and the "commodification of labor"—the two tendencies that in the Marxian scheme were supposed to generate a simultaneous increase in the social power and the mass misery of labor. On the contrary, global wars and their preparation were more powerful factors of industrial advancement and mass misery than market rule had ever been. But the demise of the world market meant that the social power and the mass misery of the world proletariat came to be distributed among its various segments far less evenly than they had been before.

Generally speaking, in the periods of war mobilization the size of the Active Industrial Army increased (both absolutely and relative to the size of the Reserve Army) in most locations of the world-economy—including countries not directly involved in the war. Moreover, the increasing "industrialization of war" in the late nineteenth and early twentieth centuries had made the cooperation of industrial recruits as important as (if not more important than) the cooperation of military recruits in determining the outcome of war efforts. The social power of labor thus grew in step with the escalation of the power struggle in the interstate system.

But global wars also absorbed a growing amount of resources and disrupted the networks of production and exchange through which resources were procured. As a consequence, the overall capabilities of the ruling classes to accommodate labor's demands decreased or did not rise as rapidly as the social power of labor. World wars thus created that combination of proletarian power and proletarian deprivation which in the Marxian scheme was supposed to bring about an intensification of the class struggle and the eventual demise of the rule of capital.

Both world wars did in fact generate global waves of class struggle. Overall strike activity declined in the opening years of the two wars only to escalate rapidly in their closing years. The resulting peaks in world labor unrest had no historical precedent, and have remained unmatched to this day. And each peak was associated with a major socialist revolution—the first with the Soviet Revolution and the second with the Chinese Revolution. Though these waves of class struggle did not bring the rule of capital to an end, they did bring about fundamental changes in the way in which that rule was exercised. These changes proceeded along two radically different and divergent trajectories which correspond quite closely to the opposite stands taken by Eduard Bernstein and V. I. Lenin in the course of the so-called Revisionist Controversy.

In one of its final resolutions, the International Socialist Congress of 1896 predicted an imminent general crisis that would put the exercise of state power on the agenda of Socialist parties. It therefore impressed upon the proletariat of all countries "the imperative necessity of learning, as class conscious citizens, how to administer the business of their respective countries for the common good." In line with this resolution, it was decided that future congresses would be open only to representatives of organizations that worked to transform the capitalist order into a socialist order and were prepared to participate in legislative and parliamentary activities. All Anarchists were thereby excluded.

The end of the old controversy between the followers of Marx and those of Bakunin marked the beginning of a new controversy among the followers of Marx themselves. While the goal of working toward the socialist transformation of the capitalist order was stated in terms sufficiently vague and ambiguous to suit all shades of opinion among Marx's followers, the very definition of a common political objective for the proletariat of all countries posed some fundamental theoretical and practical problems. Eduard Bernstein was the first to bring these problems out into the open.

Even though Bernstein has gone down in history as the Great Revisionist of Marxian thought, his declared revisionism was actually very mild, particularly in comparison to the revisionism of some of his "orthodox" opponents. In line with the principles of *scientific* socialism, he sought validation/invalidation for Marx's theses of a secular increase in the social power of labor and of a simultaneous secular increase in its misery. And like Marx, he thought that the best guide to the future of the labor movement in Continental Europe in general and in Germany in particular was the past and present of the movement in Britain. He accordingly focused his attention on trends in the latter.

Starting from these premises, he found plenty of evidence in support of the thesis of a secular increase in the social power of labor and little evidence in support of the thesis of a secular increase in mass misery. In support of the first thesis he adduced not only the significant improvements in the standards of life and work of the industrial proletariat but also the expansion and transformation of political democracy from a tool of subordination into a tool of emancipation of the working classes. Writing at the end of the Great Depression of 1873–96 and at the beginning of the Belle

Epoque of European capitalism, he saw no reason why these trends should be reversed in the foreseeable future. The liberal organizations of modern society were there to stay, and were sufficiently flexible to accommodate an indefinite increase in the social power of labor. As in the past, all that was needed was "organization and *energetic action*" (my emphasis). A socialist revolution in the sense of a revolutionary dictatorship of the proletariat, was neither necessary nor desirable (Bernstein 1961: 163-64).

Bernstein summed up his position in the slogan "The movement is everything, the goal nothing." This sounded like a provocation to Marxist reformists and revolutionaries alike. It was in fact a reformist (Karl Kautsky) who led the onslaught against Bernstein's revisionism. Kautsky argued, essentially, that all economic and political gains of the proletariat were conjunctural, that a general crisis was inevitable and indeed in the making, and that in such a crisis the bourgeoisie would try to win back forcibly whatever economic and political concessions it had had to make previously to the proletariat. Under these circumstances, everything would be lost unless the proletariat and its organizations were prepared to seize and to hold, if necessary through politically revolutionary means, the commanding heights of the state and of the economy.

Kautsky thus retained all of Marx's ambiguities concerning the relationship between the present struggles of the proletariat (the "movement" in Bernstein's slogan) and the ultimate objective of socialist revolution (the "goal"). Nevertheless, the argument that sooner or later all the achievements of the movement were going to be jeopardized in an inevitable crisis unless the organizations of the proletariat were prepared to seize state power was a short step away from the conclusion that the goal was everything and the movement nothing.

Kautsky never took this step. It was left to Lenin, who had sided with Kautsky against Bernstein, to carry Kautsky's argument to its logical conclusion. If only a socialist seizure of state power could save/expand all previous achievements of the movement, then the former had clear priority over the latter. It also followed that the achievements of the movement were deceptive. For one thing, they did not take into account the future losses that the movement, left to itself, would inevitably encounter. In addition, they only reflected one side of the proletarian condition. By adding new emphasis to the thesis of the "labor aristocracy," Lenin implicitly dismissed Marx's view that the best guide to the future of the labor movement in Continental Europe and elsewhere was the present and the past of the labor movement in Britain. The increasing social power of labor in Britain was a local and short-term phenomenon connected with Britain's position at the commanding heights of the world economy. The present and the future of the proletariat of Continental Europe in general and of the Russian Empire in particular was one of increasing mass misery and continuing political oppression, notwithstanding the presence of highly energetic and well-organized labor movements.

Two conclusions followed. First, the achievements (or for that matter the failures) of proletarian movements created the wrong kind of perceptions among their leaderships and rank and file. Consciousness of the necessity and of the possibility of socialist revolution could only develop outside the movements and had to be brought to the movements by a professional revolutionary vanguard. Second, the organizations of the movements had to be transformed into "transmission belts" capable of conveying the commands of the revolutionary vanguards to the proletarian masses. In this theorization, the movement was truly nothing, mere means, the goal everything.

Looking back at the actual evolution of the labor movement over the entire period 1896–1948, we find plenty of evidence validating either Lenin's or Bernstein's positions but very little validating the intermediate Kautskian position. It all depends where we look. Bernstein's prediction/prescription that organization and energetic action were sufficient to force/induce the ruling classes to accommodate economically and politically the secular increase in the social power of labor associated with the advancement of industry captures the essence of the trajectory of the labor movements of the Anglo-Saxon and Scandinavian worlds. Notwithstanding two world wars and a catastrophic world-economic crisis, which Bernstein failed to predict, the proletariat in these locations continued to experience an improvement in economic welfare and governmental representation commensurate to its increasingly important role in the system of social production.

The most spectacular advances occurred in Sweden and Australia. But the most significant advances from the point of view of the politics of the world-economy took place in Britain (the declining hegemonic power but still the dominant colonial power) and in the United States (the rising hegemonic power). A marginal and subordinate force in the national politics of both states in 1896, organized labor had become by 1948 the governing party of Britain and a decisive influence on the U.S. government. All this was achieved precisely along the path predicted and prescribed by Bernstein—the path, that is, of energetic and well-organized movements capable of exploiting whatever opportunity arose to transform the increasing social power of labor into greater economic welfare and better political representation. In this context, the goal of socialist revolution never became an issue, and revolutionary vanguards of the proletariat found few followers.

Yet, 1896–1948 is also the period of the greatest successes of socialist revolution. It is in this period that self-proclaimed revolutionary vanguards of the proletariat took control of the means of rule over almost half of Eurasia. Though different in many respects, the experiences of the proletariat in the Russian and former Chinese empires presented important analogies. Vigorous movements of protest (in 1905 in the Russian Empire, in 1925–27 in China) had failed to improve the conditions of existence for the proletariat. Increasing mass misery, rather than increasing social power, was the overwhelming experience of the proletariat in these locales. Moreover, the escalation of the interstate power struggle ("imperialism" in Lenin's theory of revolution) had further increased the inability of the ruling classes to provide the proletariat with minimal protection.

Under these circumstances, a vanguard of dedicated revolutionaries trained in the scientific analysis of social events, trends, and conjunctures could take advantage of the disruption of national and world power networks to carry out successful socialist revolutions. The foundation of the power of this vanguard was the impoverishment of the increasingly extensive exploited masses, regardless of their precise class locations. For increasing mass misery transformed the vast majority of the population into actual or potential members of the Industrial Reserve Army and, at the same time, prevented whoever happened to be in the Active Industrial Army at any given time from developing a separate class identity from that of other subordinate groups and classes. In this context, the movements of protest that did develop within the transient and precarious condition of the wage labor force provided neither an adequate foundation for a continuing movement, nor a direction to political action oriented toward the socialist transformation of the existing social order. The ways and means of that transformation had indeed to be developed outside of, and often in opposition to, the spontaneous movements of protest of the proletarian masses.

The most striking feature of these divergent tendencies—the development of the social power of labor in some locations and of socialist revolution against mass misery in other locations—is that, taken together, they demonstrated the historical imperviousness of the industrial proletariat to socialist-revolutionary ideologies and practices. Where the social power of the industrial proletariat was significant and growing, socialist revolution had no constituency; and where socialist revolution had a constituency, the industrial proletariat had no social power. This negative correlation between the social power of labor and its socialist revolutionary predispositions had already appeared in embryonic form at the time of the Paris Commune and, as argued in section 2 above, was probably the most important single cause of the disbanding of the First International. Faced with a choice, both theoretical and political, between a strong but reformist labor movement in Britain and a revolutionary but weak labor movement in France, Marx chose not to choose and left the issue up in the air.

As Marxism turned into a political institution, against Marx's and Engels' original intentions, a choice had to be made, particularly in view of the fact that the disjunction between the social power and the revolutionary predispositions of the proletariat was increasing instead of decreasing. Bernstein posed the problem and chose to side with the social power of labor (the "movement"); Lenin chose to side with the revolutionary predispositions that grew out of increasing mass misery (the "goal," in Bernstein's antinomy); and Kautsky, like Marx thirty years earlier, chose not to choose. This indeed was his only legitimate claim to "orthodoxy."

This choice not to choose had disastrous political implications. Whereas Bernstein's choice was validated by the subsequent successes of the labor movement in the Anglo-Saxon world and Scandinavia, and Lenin's choice by the subsequent successes of socialist revolution in the former Russian and Chinese empires, Kautsky's choice not to choose was invalidated as a political strategy by the subsequent successes of counterrevolution in central and southern Europe. For the rise of Fascism and National Socialism can be traced at least in part to the chronic inability of the relevant working-class organizations to choose between energetic reformist and energetic revolutionary action.

To be sure, this chronic inability to choose was related to the more complex social situation which labor organizations faced in these regions—a situation, that is, characterized by a combination of increasing social power of labor and of increasing mass misery rather than by the predominance of one or the other tendency. The contradiction was real and localized. This combination generated within the industrial proletariat significant revolutionary predispositions alongside more reformist predispositions—a combination that left the leadership of the movement in a permanent dilemma. Kautsky's choice not to choose, and the impressive theoretical and political apparatus that backed it up, provided plenty of justifications for a leadership that instead of tilting the balance in a specific direction, reflected passively the divisions that tore apart the movement and thus compounded political confusion and disorientation. We shall never know whether a more energetic reformist or revolutionary action on the part of German Social Democrats would have made any difference to subsequent German and world history. But just as the historical responsibilities of German Social Democracy (or for that matter of Italian Socialism) in paving the way to National Socialism and Fascism should not be belittled, they should not be exaggerated either. For the hegemonic successes of reactionary elites in seizing power in countries as diverse as Germany, Japan, and Italy had world-systemic as well as local causes.

These world-systemic causes were the joint processes of disintegration of world-market rule and escalation of the interstate power struggle outlined at the begining of this section. These processes put a premium on war preparedness, which in the twentieth century had come to mean first and foremost expansion and modernization of military-industrial complexes, on the one hand, and an exclusive or privileged access to the world-economic resources required for that expansion and modernization, on the other hand. In states affected by a structural disequilibrium between an overgrown military-industrial apparatus and a narrow domestic economic base, revanchist ideologies had a strong appeal to all kinds of social groups, including non-negligible fractions of the industrial proletariat.

Under these circumstances, the political indeterminacy engendered by the contradictory predispositions toward reform and revolution of the industrial proletariat contributed to undermine the legitimacy of organized labor, regardless of its actual role in compounding the indeterminacy. Whatever its causes, the rise of National Socialism in Germany became the decisive event in precipitating a new round of generalized war and class struggle. It was in the course of this round that organized labor became a decisive political influence on the great powers of the Anglo-Saxon world and that the domain of socialist-revolutionary regimes came to include almost half of Eurasia.

It is important to notice that this prodigious expansion of the political power of elected and self-appointed representatives of the industrial proletariat took place in the context of an almost complete disappearance of autonomous revolutionary predispositions on the part of the industrial proletariat itself. Nowhere during and after World War II did the industrial proletariat attempt to take state power into its own hands through "communes" or "soviets"—not even in defeated countries, as it had done in France in 1871, in Russia in 1917, in Germany and Austria-Hungary in 1919–20. The expansion of the domain of socialist-revolutionary regimes was essentially due to armies defeating other armies—a proletarian version of Gramsci's "Piedmontese Function" (Gramsci 1971: 104–5).

In Eastern Europe, Communist regimes were established by the Soviet Army, substantively if not formally. Elsewhere, as in Yugoslavia, Albania and, most important, China, communist regimes were established by indigenous armies raised and controlled by revolutionary political elites and cadres who had taken the lead in the struggle of national liberation against Axis Powers. Even in Italy and France, where Communist parties won hegemony over significant fractions of the industrial proletariat, this hegemony was largely the result of previous leadership in the armed struggle against German occupation. Rejected by the labor movement of core countries, socialist revolution found a new and highly responsive constituency in national liberation movements.

4. U.S. Hegemony and the Remaking of the World Labor Movement

In 1948 a simple extrapolation of the main social and political trends of the previous half a century pointed toward an imminent termination of the rule of capital. Each round of generalized war and class struggle had resulted in major advances of socialist revolution in the periphery and semiperiphery of the world-economy and in major advances in the social and political power of the industrial proletariat in core countries. Were the trends not reversed, the only question that remained open was not whether capitalism would survive but by what particular mix of reforms and revolutions it would die.

But the trends were reversed, and in the next twenty years capitalism experienced a new "golden age" of unprecedented expansion. The single most important development in this reversal was the pacification of interstate relations and the reconstruction of the world market under U.S. hegemony. Up to 1968, the reconstruction of the world market remained partial and heavily dependent on U.S. military and financial capabilities. Then, between 1968 and 1973, the collapse of the Bretton Woods system and the defeat of the United States in Vietnam showed that these capabilities in and by themselves were no longer either sufficient or necessary for the ongoing process of world-market reconstruction. For it is precisely from 1973 onward that the world market seems to have become within limits an "autonomous force" that no one state (the United States included) can control. In concert, states, corporations, and administering agencies can, and do, construct and manage the limits of the world market, but not without difficulty and unintended consequences. As a matter of fact, it would seem that at no time in capitalist history has the rule of the world market *per se* approached Marx's limiting ideal type as much as it has in the last fifteen to twenty years.

Today, the social foundations of the world market are quite different from what they were in the nineteenth century. At the end of the war, the United States did not set out to reestablish the same kind of world market that had collapsed over the previous fifty years. Quite apart from the historical lessons of that collapse and the structural differences between nineteenth-century British capitalism and twentieth-century U.S. capitalism, to be discussed presently, the power and influence gained by organized labor in the United States and Britain and the successes of socialist revolution in Eurasia made such a reestablishment neither feasible nor advisable. The most enlightened factions of the U.S. ruling classes had long understood that no return to the strictly bourgeois order of the nineteenth century was possible. A new world order could not be built on the social power and aspirations of the world bourgeoisie alone; it also had to include as large a fraction of the world proletariat as, in their view, was possible.

A most important aspect of this strategy was U.S. support for "decolonization" and for an expansion/consolidation of the system of sovereign states. Like Wilson before him, Franklin D. Roosevelt implicitly shared Lenin's view that the struggle over territory and population among core capitalist states was a negative-sum game that created a favorable environment for socialist revolutions and the ultimate demise of the world rule of capital. If the tide of socialist revolution in Eurasia were to be stopped before it was too late, this struggle had to be brought to an end and the right to self-determination of the weaker fractions of the world bourgeoisie and of the world proletariat had to be acknowledged.

A secondary but none the less highly important aspect of President Roosevelt's and his successor's world-hegemonic strategy was that it aimed at accommodating the social power of labor at home and expanding it abroad. This policy had a number of advantages for the coalition of interests that had come to rule the United States. From the point of view of corporate capital, it would create in Europe and elsewhere "domestic" mass markets similar to the one already existing in the United States and thus pave the way for its further transnational expansion. From the point of view of organized labor, it reduced the threat of competitive pressures originating in the lower standards of returns for effort obtaining almost everywhere else in the world. Last and most important, from the point of view of the government, a policy of accommodation at home and expansion abroad of the social power of labor meant that the United States could present itself, and be widely perceived, as the bearer of the interests, not just of capital, but of labor as well. It was this policy, together with support for decolonization, that transformed U.S. military and financial supremacy into a true world hegemony.[3]

U.S. military and financial power thus became the vehicle through which the ideology and practice of the primacy of the movement over the goal, typical of the U.S. labor movement, was exported as far as that power reached. The transplant was most successful in those defeated states (West Germany and Japan) where the U.S. Army by itself or in collusion with its allies held absolute governmental power and, at the same time, industrialization had proceeded far enough to provide organized labor with a firm social base. Even where it was most successful, however, this restructuring of class relations from above by a foreign power would have come to nothing were it not followed, as it was, by the reconstruction of world-market rule and a rapid spread of the structures of accumulation on which the social power of labor in the United States rested.

In the previous section, the U.S. labor movement was dealt with as part of a wider Anglo-Saxon model in which the "movement" had primacy over the "goal." Yet, in the interwar period the U.S. labor movement had come to exemplify better than the labor movement in any other country the social power that the accumulation of capital puts in the hands of labor. Elsewhere in that world and in Scandinavia—particularly in Britain, Australia, and Sweden—strong labor movements had found expression in the rise of labor parties, which remained under the control of the movement but could act as substitutes for and complements of the movement if and when the need arose. In the United States no such development had taken place. At most an existing party had become organized labor's principal political representation. The movement went forward or foundered as its capabilities of self-mobilization and self-organization succeeded or failed.

These capabilities were the unintended consequence of the structural transformations undergone by U.S. capital over the previous half a century. Also in this respect, the Great Depression of 1873–96 had been a decisive turning point. It was in that period that U.S. capital had created vertically integrated, bureaucratically managed structures of accumulation that corresponded to the full development of Marx's "production of relative surplus value" (cf. Chandler 1977, Aglietta 1979).

As painstakingly demonstrated by Harry Braverman (1974), the creation of these structures of accumulation was associated with the recomposition of labor processes such that as the processes became more complex the skills required of each participant became fewer and less difficult to master (his "de-skilling"). This reworking of the technical division of labor undermined the social power of the comparatively small class of wage workers (primarily craftworkers) who controlled the skills necessary to perform the complex tasks. However, the decreasing social power of craftworkers was only one side of the coin. The other side was the greater social power that accrued to the comparatively much larger class of waged operatives who came to perform the simpler ("semiskilled") tasks.

"De-skilling" was in fact a double-edged sword which eased the valorization of capital in one direction only to make it more problematic in another direction. The valorization of capital was eased because it was made less dependent on the knowledge and skills of craftworkers. But this reduced dependence on the knowledge and skills of craftworkers was associated with a major expansion of managerial hierarchies (Galbraith's "technostructures") whose valorization depended on the speed of production processes and, therefore, on the willingness of a large mass of operatives to cooperate with one another and with management in keeping production flows moving at the required speed. This greater importance of the productive effort of a large mass of operatives for the valorization of complex and expensive technostructures provided the social power of labor with a new and broader foundation.

This new and broader foundation became manifest for the first time in the course of the long wave of strikes and labor unrest that unfolded in the United States between the middle 1930s and the late 1940s. The strike wave began as a spontaneous response of the rank and file of the industrial proletariat to the attempts by capital to shift onto labor the burdens of the Great Slump of the early 1930s.[4] The main and indeed the only preexisting organization of the industrial proletariat of any significance (the AFL) did nothing to initiate the strike wave. It became active in organizing and leading the movement only when the latter had proved capable of standing on its own and of generating alternative organizational structures, which became the CIO.

The struggles were most successful in the period of war mobilization and, as argued earlier, war mobilization tended to inflate the social power of labor. Yet, McCarthyism notwithstanding, most of the wartime gains were consolidated in the period of war demobilization. For a decade or two the U.S. industrial proletariat enjoyed unprecedented and unparalleled economic welfare and political influence. But the social power of labor in the United States was also contained. The most effective forms of struggle were delegitimated, conflict was routinized, and the pace of U.S. corporate expansion abroad experienced a sudden acceleration.

U.S. corporate capital's predisposition to expand its operations transnationally long preceded the strike wave of the 1930s and 1940s. It was built into the processes of vertical integration and of bureaucratization of management which brought it into being in the late nineteenth century and constituted its essential form of expansion. In the 1930s and 1940s, however, the escalation of the interstate power struggle seriously hampered U.S. direct investment in Europe and its colonies precisely at a time when the increasing social power of labor at home was making expansion abroad more profitable and urgent. It should be no surprise, therefore, that as soon as the U.S. government had created conditions highly favorable for corporate expansion in Western Europe (primarily through the Marshall Plan), U.S. capital seized the opportunity and set out to remake Europe in its image and to its likeness.

U.S. corporate capital was not the only actor involved in this remaking of Europe. European governments and businesses joined eagerly in the enterprise, in part to catch up with the new standards of power and wealth set by the United States and in part to meet the competition brought into their midst by the U.S. corporate invasion. The result was an unprecedented expansion of production facilities which embodied the new structures of accumulation pioneered in the United States in the first half of the century. With the new structures of accumulation came also a massive increase in the social power of European labor.

This massive increase was signaled in the late 1960s and early 1970s by a strike wave that presented important analogies with the U.S. strike wave of the 1930s and 1940s. First, this wave also was largely based on the capabilities of self-mobilization and self-organization of the rank and file of the industrial proletariat. Preexisting labor organizations, regardless of their ideological orientation, played no role in initiating the struggles and became involved in leading and organizing the militancy only when the latter had proved capable of standing on its own and of generating alternative organizational structures. Often, the new movements and labor organizations came into conflict with one another as the latter tried to impose on the former their own political objectives and the former struggled to retain its autonomy from objectives that transcended the proletarian condition.

Second, the foundation of the self-mobilization and self-organization of the industrial proletariat was wholly internal to the proletarian condition. Self-mobilization was a spontaneous and collective response to the attempts of capital to shift the intensifying competitive pressures of the world-economy onto labor by curtailing rewards for effort (primarily by demanding greater effort). And self-organization was the use of the technical organization of the labor process so as to coordinate scattered acts of insurgency.

Third, the movement was highly successful, not only in the pursuit of its immediate objectives, but in inducing the ruling classes to accommodate the social power demonstrated by labor in the struggles. Between 1968 and 1973, rewards for effort skyrocketed throughout Western Europe, bringing them close to North American standards. At the same time or shortly afterward, the formal or substantive restrictions on the civil and political rights of the industrial proletariat still in force in many Western European countries began to crumble.

Finally, the accommodation of the social power of labor was slowed and then halted by reorienting the expansion of production processes toward more peripheral locations. Up to 1968, the transnational expansion of production processes, as measured for example by direct investment abroad, was primarily a U.S.-based phenomenon, while that by European-based firms was a residual of their earlier colonial operations and experiences. Capitalist enterprises originating in small and wealthy countries, such as Sweden and Switzerland, had also engaged in this kind of expansion but the enterprises of the larger and more dynamic core countries, such as Germany and Japan, were conspicuous for their absence in the construction of transnational networks of production and distribution.

Then, between 1968 and 1973, there occurred a sudden acceleration in direct foreign investment in which previous laggards, Japan in particular, played a leading role. By 1988, control over transnational production and distribution networks had become a common feature of core capital of all nationalities, with Japanese capital close to overtaking U.S. capital in the extent and scope of the networks controlled. Japan's leadership in the sudden acceleration of direct foreign investment in the 1970s and 1980s has not been just a matter of exceptionally high rates of growth. Accompanying, and indeed underlying, these exceptionally high rates of growth was an anticipation of, and a prompt adjustment to, world-economic trends in labor-capital relations. As soon as domestic strike activity and labor costs began to rise, Japanese capital promptly relocated abroad the production processes that were most dependent on an ample supply of cheap labor. What's more, at least in its initial stages the transnational expansion of Japanese capital, unlike that of US capital, was oriented primarily towards reducing costs rather than expanding revenues (cf. Ozawa 1979).

Japanese leadership in the transnational expansion of capital of the 1970s and 1980s was built on the anticipation of the difficulties created for the accumulation of capital by the generalization of the structures of corporate capitalism to the entire core zone. As long as corporate capitalism was almost exclusively a U.S. phenomenon, U.S. corporations could pick and choose among a wide range of locations where to seek the valorization of their managerial hierarchies. This lack of competition was the single most important reason why U.S. corporate capital in the 1950s and most of the 1960s could simultaneously expand its productive base abroad and at home, accommodate the social power of labor that went with that expansion, and increase the mass of profit under its control. By the late 1960s and early 1970s, the greatly expanded managerial hierarchies of U.S. capital were no longer alone in seeking valorization outside their original domain. Western European and Japanese capitalist enterprises had developed the same kinds of capabilities and propensities, while the number of locations offering comparable opportunities of profitable expansion had decreased. Western Europe, which had been a prime location for the valorization of U.S. capital externally, was itself seeking a profitable outlet for its own overgrown technostructures. Opportunities for foreign direct investment in the rest of the world were narrowly constrained, either by centralized state controls over production and distribution (as in all Communist countries) or by mass misery (as in most third world countries), or by a combination of the two.

The cost-cutting race of the 1970s and 1980s has its deeper roots in this situation of overcrowding—that is, a situation in which too many corporate structures "chased" too few locations offering profitable opportunities of expansion. In the 1970s, attempts by states and corporations to sustain the expansion of productive facilities and to accommodate the increasing social power of labor that went with it simply resulted in an accentuation of inflationary pressures. These pressures, in turn, enhanced the profitability of cost-cutting and the attractiveness of speculative activities which, in the 1980s, have accordingly drawn to them increasing monetary resources and entrepreneurial energies.

Financial speculation and cost-cutting activities are thus reflections of the growing inability of corporate capital to adjust to the increasing social power of labor that goes with corporate capital's own expansion. Their main impact has been a limited but nonetheless very real spread of mass misery to the core zone. The phenomenon has taken different forms: falling real wages (primarily in the United States), rising unemployment (primarily in Western Europe), and an increasing effort-price of proletarian incomes in almost all core locations.

This increase in mass misery has not been associated with a proportionate decrease in the social power of labor. Financial speculation reflects the emergence of an incompatibility between corporate expansion and the increasing social power of labor. It cannot stop the latter without stopping the former. Its main effect is to undermine the social consensus on which the rule of capital has rested since World War II.

As for cost-cutting activities, they have taken three main forms: (a) a substitution of cheaper for more expensive sources of wage labor *within* each and every core state—the feminization of the waged labor force being the most important aspect of this substitution, and the more extensive use of first-generation, often illegal, immigrant labor its secondary aspect; (b) a substitution of cheaper for more expensive sources of wage labor *across* state boundaries, particularly between core and more peripheral regions— plant relocation and substitution of imports for domestic production being the most important aspects of this substitution; (c) a substitution of intellectual and scientific labor power for proletarian labor power in production processes—automation and the use of science-based technologies being its most important aspects.

The first two kinds of substitution have been by far the most important in spreading mass misery to the proletariat of core countries. Yet, neither of them involves a reduction in the overall social power of the world proletariat. What they do involve is a transfer of social power from one segment of the world proletariat to another segment. Substitution within core states transfers social power from male to female and from native to immigrant members of the industrial proletariat; and substitution across state boundaries transfers social power from the proletariat of one state to the proletariat of another state. Either way, social power changes hands but remains in the hands of the industrial proletariat.

Automation and science-based technologies, in contrast, involve a reduction in the social power of the proletariat as presently constituted. By transferring control over the quality and quantity of production from subordinate wage workers to managers, intellectuals and scientists, this kind of substitution transfers social power from substantively proletarianized workers to workers who, at best, are proletarianized only in the formal sense of working for a wage or salary. However, the stronger this tendency and the larger the size of the managerial and scientific labor force in the overall economy of production processes, the stronger also the tendency for capital to subject this labor force to its rule, and thus make its proletarianization more substantive than it has been thus far. In this case, therefore, there is a transfer of social power out of the hands of the industrial proletariat, but only as a premise to a future enlargement of its size and power.

It follows that the deteriorating living standards of the proletariat in core countries has been associated not so much with a loss as with a redistribution of social power within its present and future ranks. Social power and mass misery are no longer as polarized in different segments of the world proletariat as they were in the middle of the twentieth century. Mass misery has begun to spread to the proletariat of the core, while social power has begun to trickle down to the proletariat of the periphery and semiperiphery. In short, we are approaching the scenario envisaged by Marx and Engels in the *Manifesto*—a scenario in which the social power and the mass misery of labor affect the same human material rather than different and separate segments of the world proletariat.

To be sure, social power and material deprivation are still distributed extremely unevenly among the various components of the world proletariat. Insofar as we can tell, this distribution will remain very uneven for a long time to come. Yet, the tendency of the first half of the twentieth century toward a spatial polarization of the social power and mass misery of labor in different and separate regions of the world-economy has begun to be reversed.

Between 1948 and 1968, the social power previously enjoyed almost exclusively by the industrial proletariat of the Anglo-Saxon world spread to the industrial proletariat of the entire core zone, which had come to include most of Western Europe and Japan, while mass misery continued to be the predominant experience of the proletarianized and semi-proletarianized masses of the third world. From circa 1968, however, this polarization became counterproductive for the further expansion of corporate capital. In core regions, the enlarged social power of labor began to interfere seriously with the command of capital over production processes. In peripheral regions, the enlarged mass misery of labor undermined the legitimacy of the rule of capital, impoverished markets, and interfered with the productive mobilization of large segments of the proletariat.

Faced with these opposite and mutually reinforcing obstacles to its further expansion, corporate capital has been trying ever since to overcome its difficulties by bringing the mass misery of the proletariat of the semi-periphery and periphery of the world-economy to bear upon the social power of labor in the core. The attempt has been eased by the on-going reconstruction of the world market which, from 1968 onward, has become increasingly independent of specifically U.S. interests and power. This reflects, among other things, the ever-widening and deepening transnational organization of production and distribution processes through which corporate capital regardless of nationality has been trying to bypass, contain, and undermine the social power of labor in the core.

The result has been a major reshuffling of the human material that constitutes the Active and Reserve Industrial armies. In comparison with twenty years ago, a far larger proportion of the world Active Industrial Army is now located in the periphery and semiperiphery of the world-economy, while the Active Army in the core contains a larger number of female and immigrant recruits in its lower ranks and of formally proletarianized intellectuals and scientists in its upper ranks. This reshuffling has put considerable pressure on the native male workers of the core employed in the lower and middle ranks of the Active Army to accept lower standards of reward for effort or else be squeezed out of the Active Army.

Resistance against this deterioration of living standards in the core has thus far been rather weak and ineffectual, mainly because the segments of the industrial proletariat that have experienced it most directly have also been affected by a loss of social power, while the segments that have been gaining social power have not yet experienced a major deterioration in living standards. In the case of the women and immigrants who have come to occupy the lower ranks of the industrial proletariat, two circumstances have softened the impact of the deterioration. On the one hand, standards of reward for effort in their previous occupations were in many instances even lower than the standards obtaining in the lower ranks of the Active Industrial Army to which they have been recruited. On the other hand, often they still consider their rewards as a supplement to other sources of income and their efforts as temporary additions to their usual work load. Low rewards for effort are thus borne with greater patience than, one would imagine, they would be if rewards were perceived as the sole or principal source of income and if the efforts were perceived as a permanent addition to their usual work load.

Both circumstances are inherently transitory. Over time, standards of rewards for effort are formed by present rather than past conditions. In addition, the more widespread becomes the use of female and immigrant labor in the lower ranks of the Active Industrial Army, the more low rewards turn into the main source of income and high effort turns into a lifetime condition. As this happens, aquiescence gives way to open rebellion in which the social power of women and immigrants is turned against the rising tide of mass misery in the core.

Even in the 1970s and 1980s, women and immigrants in core states have shown a strong predisposition to rebel and make use of their social power; but we have yet to see a major wave of industrial conflict focused specifically on their grievances. If and when it occurs, this kind of wave will interact positively and negatively with movements of protest originating in the upper ranks of the Active Industrial Army.

These upper ranks are increasingly occupied by intellectuals and scientists who are taking over an ever widening range of productive tasks. For now, they are the main beneficiaries of the on-going cost-cutting race which inflates the demand for their labor power and provides them with comparatively inexpensive luxuries. But the more their weight in the cost structure of capital increases, the more they will be targeted as the main object of the cost-cutting race. At that point, also, these upper strata of the Active Industrial Army can be expected to mobilize their social power in movements of protest aimed at preventing mass misery from spreading to their own ranks.

These are the movements of the future of the core. But in the semiperiphery the future has already begun. The 1980s have witnessed major explosions of labor unrest in countries as different as Poland, South Africa, and South Korea—just to mention the most significant episodes of a new rising tide of industrial conflict. Notwithstanding the radically different political regimes and social structures of these countries, these explosions present important common features, some of which resemble those attributed earlier to the waves of class struggle of the 1930s and 1940s in the United States and of the late 1960s and early 1970s in Western Europe.

In all instances, industrial conflict has been largely based on the capabilities of self-mobilization and self-organization of the rank and file of the industrial proletariat. The foundation of these capabilities has been wholly internal to the proletarian condition and has consisted of a fundamental disequilibrium between the new social power and the old mass misery of the industrial proletariat of these countries.

The resemblances in these respects are striking. Nevertheless, the differences between this latest wave and the earlier waves have been as significant as the similarities. These movements have been as hard to repress as the earlier ones; but they have been far more difficult to accommodate. The reason lies not in the grievances themselves, which are far more basic than the grievances of the earlier waves, but in the limited capabilities of states and capital in the semiperiphery to adjust to even the most basic of grievances. The result might well be a situation of endemic social strife of the kind envisaged by Marx and Engels in the *Manifesto*.

5. The Crisis of Marxism in World-Historical Perspective

The argument that the predictions of the *Manifesto* concerning the world labor movement might be more relevant for the next fifty to sixty years than they have been for the last ninety to one hundred years may seem to be contradicted by the current crisis of organized labor and Marxist organizations. There is no denying that over the last fifteen or twenty years labor unions, working-class parties, and states ruled by Socialist governments, particularly of the Communist variety, have all been under considerable pressure to restructure themselves and change their orientation or face decline. This pressure, however, is not at all incompatible with the argument developed here. On the contrary, it provides further evidence in its support.

Like all other social organizations, proletarian organizations (whether Marxist or not) pursue strategies and have structures that reflect the historical circumstances under which they have come into existence, and most continue to retain the same sort of strategy and structure long after the circumstances of their origins are over with. The proletarian ideologies and organizations that are now under pressure to change or face decline all reflect the historical circumstances typical of the first half of the twentieth century—a period in which the capitalist world-economy departed in fundamental ways from the scenario sketched in the *Manifesto*. To the extent that the capitalist world-economy once again begins to match more closely than before that scenario, it is only to be expected that all organizations whose strategies and structures reflect the historical circumstances of a previous epoch would be challenged fundamentally and be faced with the prospect of decline. Some may be able to stave off the decline, even prosper, through a simple change in strategy. Others can attain the same result but only through a process of thorough self-restructuring. And others again can only decline, no matter what they do.

More specifically, Marx had assumed that market rule would constantly reshuffle within and across the various locations of the capitalist world-economy the increasing social power and the increasing mass misery of labor. In actual fact, for a long time this did not happen. In the first half of the twentieth century the escalation of the interstate power struggle first impaired and then totally disrupted the operation of the world market. The social power and the mass misery of labor increased faster than ever before but in polarized fashion, with the proletariat in some regions experiencing primarily an increase in social power, and the proletariat in other regions experiencing primarily an increase in mass misery. As Marx had predicted, this accentuation of the tendencies toward an increasing social power and an increasing mass misery of labor gave a tremendous impulse to the spread of proletarian struggles, ideologies, and organizations. But the polarized fashion in which the two tendencies materialized made proletarian struggles, ideologies, and organizations develop along trajectories which Marx had neither predicted nor advocated.

The assumption that the two tendencies would affect the same human material across the space of the capitalist world-economy was an essential ingredient in Marx's theory of the socialist transformation of the world. Only under this assumption would the everyday struggles of the world proletariat be inherently revolutionary in the sense that they would bring to bear on states and capital a social power which the latter could neither repress nor accommodate. Socialist revolution was the long-term, large-scale process whereby the ensemble of these struggles would force upon the world bourgeoisie an order based on consensus and cooperation instead of coercion and competition.

Within this process the role of revolutionary vanguards, if any, was supposed to be moral and educational rather than political. According to the *Manifesto*, truly revolutionary vanguards ("communists") were not supposed to form separate parties opposed to other working-class parties; they were not supposed to develop interests of their own separate and apart from those of the proletariat as a whole; and they were not supposed to set up sectarian principles by which to shape and mould the proletarian movement. Rather, they were supposed to limit themselves to express and represent *within* proletarian struggles the common interests of the entire world proletariat and of the movement as a whole (see the passage quoted above). The most striking fact about this list of what revolutionary vanguards were not supposed to do is that it is a list of what Marxists actually did do in becoming collective historical agents.

The formation at the end of the nineteenth century of separate parties competing with and often opposed to other working-class parties was the first thing that Marxists did. As a matter of fact, this formation of separate political parties marks the very act of birth of Marxism as effective historical agency and shared ideological identity. Soon thereafter, the Revisionist Controversy purged Marxism of the idea that the movement of concrete proletarian struggles had primacy over the principles (socialist or not) set up by revolutionary vanguards. This development was a tacit invitation to set up particular principles defining criteria of proletarianism and, hence, as working guidelines for a vanguard's shaping and moulding of actual proletarian movements—something that happened right away. When one version of this way of proceeding brought to Marxism its first territorial base (the Russian Empire), the Leninist theory of the supremacy of the revolutionary vanguard over the movement became the core of Marxist orthodoxy.

Finally, having acquired a territorial domain, Marxism as an orthodoxy developed interests of its own—interests not necessarily nor evidently coincident with those imputable to the world proletariat. The internecine struggles that followed the seizure of state power in the Russian Empire redefined Marxism as coercive rule (of the party over the state and of the state over civil society) aimed not at achieving proletarian liberation as such but at keeping up or catching up with the wealth and power of the core states of the capitalist world-economy. This strategy turned the USSR into a superpower and helped bring about a phenomenal expansion of the territorial domain of Marxist rule. Coercive rule plus industrialization became the new core of orthodoxy.

Notwithstanding this progressive negation of Marx's legacy, Marxism continued to claim representation of the common interests of the entire world proletariat and world labor movement. This claim, however, was increasingly emptied of substance by a constant redefinition of the common interests of the world proletariat to match the power interests of Marxist organizations (states, parties, unions). Right from the start, the common interests of the world proletariat were redefined, one, to exclude the material interests of those segments of the world proletariat (so-called labor aristocracies) that rejected the necessary role of Marxist parties in the pursuit of their emancipation and, two, to include the power interests of Marxist organizations regardless of their participation in actual proletarian struggles. Then, as Marxist organizations came to include the USSR, the common interests of the world proletariat were redefined to give priority to the consolidation of Marxist power in the USSR and of the USSR in the state system. Finally, as the USSR became a superpower engaged in a struggle for world-hegemony with the United States, the common interests of the world proletariat were redefined once again to match the interests of the USSR in that struggle.

This trajectory of successive and cumulative negations of Marx's legacy by individuals, groups, and organizations who, nonetheless, continued to claim allegiance to that legacy, does not describe a "betrayal" of Marxism, whatever that might mean. Rather, it describes Marxism for what it is, a historical formation that conforms to the actual unfolding of the Marxian legacy under circumstances unforeseen by that legacy. Or to rephrase, Marxism was made by *bona fide* followers of Marx but under historical circumstances that were neither prefigured for them nor of their own making.

The escalation of the interstate power struggle and the concomitant breakdown of world-market rule imposed upon Marx's followers the historical necessity of choosing between alternative strategies which for Marx were not alternatives at all. As argued in section 3 above, the choice in question was between developing organic links with the segments of the world proletariat that experienced most directly and systematically the tendency toward increasing mass misery, on the one hand, or developing organic links with the segments of the world proletariat that experienced most directly and systematically the tendency toward increasing social power, on the other hand. The choice was imposed by the increasing division of the two tendencies over the space of the world-economy. Marx thought, and hoped, that this division, already observable in embryonic form in his own days, would decrease over time. Instead, the escalation of the interstate power struggle strengthened each tendency and increased their spatial division. Hence the necessity to choose, and to choose promptly.

When Bernstein raised this issue and proposed to develop organic links with the stronger segments of the world proletariat, Marxists almost unanimously rejected his proposal, regardless of their revolutionary or reformist predispositions. The actual reasons for this almost unanimous rejection, which set the course of Marxism for decades to come, fall beyond the scope of this essay. All we need to point out is that they can be imputed to motivations that in no way contradict the letter and the spirit of the Marxian legacy.

Developing organic links with the weaker rather than with the stronger fractions of the world proletariat presented a double advantage for Marxists. First, it appealed to their sense of moral outrage at the mass misery of the world proletariat, which no doubt had been a major motivation for many of them to follow in Marx's footsteps. Second, it appealed to their sense of self-esteem—the sense, that is, that there was something that they could personally do to overcome the mass misery of the world proletariat, which no doubt also played a role in inducing them to engage in working-class politics.

Bernstein's choice was disadvantageous from both points of view. If the accumulation of capital provided the proletariat with the social power necessary to stave off mass misery, Marxists—or at least most of them—were left without motivation or function: moral outrage was unjustified because mass misery was a passing phenomenon and self-esteem was out of place because the proletariat had all the power it needed to emancipate itself. It is plausible to assume that this was an unstated but important reason why Bernstein's "choice" was rejected and historical Marxism was constituted both theoretically and practically on the foundation of the increasing mass misery of labor rather than on its increasing social power.

Whatever the motivations, this was a fateful decision, not just for Marxism, but for the world proletariat, the world labor movement, and the capitalist world-system. It imposed on Marxists a double substitution which greatly enhanced their power to transform the world but also made them depart more and more radically from the letter and spirit of the Marxian legacy. At first, it imposed on Marxists the historical necessity of substituting organizations of their own making for the mass organizations that reflected the spontaneous acts of revolt of the proletariat and other subordinate groups and classes. Then, once in power, it imposed on

Marxist organizations the historical necessity of substituting themselves for the organizations of the bourgeoisie and other dominant groups and classes in performing the unpleasant governmental tasks which the latter had been unable or unwilling to do.

The two substitutions (the first associated primarily with the name of Lenin, and the second primarily with the name of Stalin) complemented one another in the sense that the first prepared the second and the second brought to completion, as best as the actors involved could, the work initiated by the first. But whatever their mutual relations, both substitutions were rooted in the previous decision of Marxists to choose as the social foundation of revolutionary theory and action the increasing mass misery rather than the increasing social power of labor. Increasing mass misery was a necessary condition for the success of Lenin's strategy of the revolutionary seizure of state power. But as soon as state power had been seized, mass misery turned into a serious constraint on what Lenin and his successors could do with that power.

The inability or unwillingness of previous ruling classes to provide basic protection (military protection in the first place) to the proletariat and other subordinate groups and classes in a situation of escalating interstate violence had been the primary factor of their downfall. Marxist organizations could thus hope to stay in power only by providing the proletariat and other subordinate groups and classes with better protection than that provided by previous ruling groups. In practice, this meant—or so it seemed to all actors involved in the consolidation of Marxist power— catching up or at least keeping up with the military-industrial complexes of the great powers of the state system.

The alleviation of mass misery was accordingly subordinated to the pursuit of this objective. Since military-industrial backwardness had been a major, if not the major cause, of the increasing mass misery of the proletariat in the Russian Empire, it seemed quite reasonable to those involved in the consolidation of Marxist power in the USSR to assume that the alleviation of mass misery itself would begin with heavy industrialization. This assumption, however, did not seem so reasonable to a large number of Soviet subjects (including a great variety of proletarian subjects) whose ways of life were disrupted by the stepping up of heavy industrialization under conditions of mass misery. Given this opposition, coercive rule became the necessary complement of heavy industrialization.

The success of the USSR in becoming one of the two superpowers of the interstate system and, at the same time, in actually alleviating the chronic mass misery of its proletarian subjects turned coercive rule *cum* industrialization into the new core of Marxist theory and practice. With this new transformation Marxism became even more closely identified than before with the mass misery of the world proletariat, and thereby enhanced its hegemonic capabilities in the periphery and semiperiphery of the world-economy. But, for that very reason, it lost most if not all of its residual appeal for those segments of the world proletariat whose predominant experience was not increasing mass misery but increasing social power.

The rejection of Marxism by the proletariat of core countries and the suppression of actual proletarian struggles in the theory and practice of historical Marxism went hand in hand. The more historical Marxism came to be identified with increasing mass misery and with the bloody struggles through which Marxist organizations attempted to overcome the powerlessness that went with mass misery, the more it become alien, nay, repugnant to the proletarians of core countries. And, conversely, the more proletarian organizations based on the increasing social power of labor in core countries succeeded in obtaining a share of the power and wealth of their respective states, the more they came to be perceived and presented by Marxists as subordinate and corrupt members of the dominant social bloc that ruled the world.

This mutual antagonism was a historical development which no one had willed or, for that matter, anticipated. Once in place, however, it provided the world bourgeoisie with a valuable ideological weapon in the struggle to reconstitute its tottering rule. As argued in section 4, the establishment of U.S. hegemony after World War II relied heavily on the claim that the experience of the U.S. proletariat could be duplicated on a world scale. Let the expansion of corporate capitalism proceed unfettered—it was claimed—and the entire world proletariat will experience sufficient social power to eliminate mass misery from its ranks.

As we now know, this claim (like all hegemonic claims) was half true and half fraudulent. As promised, the global expansion of corporate capitalism, which followed from and secured the establishment of U.S. hegemony, did in fact spread the social power of labor to the entire core, most of the semiperiphery, and parts of the periphery of the world-economy. And, as promised, the segment of the world proletariat with sufficient social power in its hands to stave off mass misery has expanded, if not in relative terms, certainly in absolute terms.

But the claim that the world labor movement could be remade to the image of the labor movement in the United States has turned out to be also half fraudulent. The increase in the social power of labor has not resulted in a proportionate decrease in the mass misery of labor, as had happened in the United States. The more corporate capitalism expanded, the less capable it became of accommodating all the social power that its own expansion put in the hands of labor. As a consequence, expansion has slowed down and the cost-cutting race of the 1970s and 1980s has set in.

The unraveling of the fraudulent aspects of U.S. hegemony has been a major factor in precipitating its crisis in the late 1960s and early 1970s. Yet, neither organized labor nor Marxist organizations have been able to take advantage of the new situation. On the contrary, both of them have been affected by a crisis as structural as that of U.S. hegemony.

The previous strength of organized labor in core countries was rooted in a situation in which a particular segment of the proletariat had considerable social power while states and capital had the capability of accommodating that power. Organized labor, as presently constituted, developed and expanded by delivering social peace to states and capital and greater returns for effort to its proletarian constituencies. The on-going cost-cutting race, however, has made states and capital more reluctant or less capable to grant labor greater returns for effort and has transferred social power into the hands of proletarian segments (women, immigrants, foreign workers, etc.) with whom existing labor organizations have weak or no organic links. Organized labor has thus lost its previous social function or its social base or both.

The strength of Marxist organizations, in contrast, was rooted in a situation in which their proletarian constituencies had little social power and in which states and capital were incapable of providing such constituencies with minimal protection. Marxist organizations, as presently constituted, grew on the basis of their capability of providing such constituencies with a better protection than previous ruling classes had been able or willing to provide. However, the strategy of keeping up and catching up with the most powerful military-industrial complexes of the interstate system, through which Marxist organizations consolidated and expanded their power, was vitiated by a fundamental contradiction.

On the one hand, this strategy required that, wittingly or unwittingly, Marxist organizations put in the hands of their proletarian constitutencies a social power comparable to the social power enjoyed by the proletariat of the core. Over time, this increasing social power was bound to interfere with the capability of Marxist organizations to pursue interests of their own at the expense of their proletarian constituencies. The longer they waited to adjust their strategies and structure to the increasing social power of their proletarian constituencies, the more serious the subsequent adjustment would have to be.

The reconstruction of world-market rule under U.S. hegemony has aggravated this contradiction in more than one way. Interstate relations came to be pacified and war as a means of territorial expansion was delegitimated. This change undermined the capability of Marxist organizations to mobilize consent among their proletarian constituencies for a strategy of coercive industrialization. In the situation of generalized preparation for war and of actual war of the 1930s and 1940s, this strategy probably reflected a genuine and deeply felt proletarian interest. But with the establishment of U.S. hegemony it came more and more to reflect the self-serving interests of Marxist organizations and of their political clienteles. At the same time, the growing division of labor in the rest of the world-economy associated with the reconstruction of market rule heightened the comparative disadvantage of coercive industrialization in the race to keep up with the standards of power and wealth set by core capitalist states. As a consequence, Marxist states became increasingly incapable of keeping up with those standards or of adjusting to the increasing social power of their proletarian subjects or both.

The crises of organized labor and of Marxist organizations are thus two sides of the same coin. The crisis of organized labor is due primarily to its structural inability to stop the spread of mass misery to the proletariat of the core, while the crisis of Marxist organizations is due primarily to their structural inability to prevent the spread of social power to their actual or prospective proletarian constituencies. But the crisis is the same because each kind of proletarian organization is ill-equipped to cope with a situation in which labor has greater social power than existing economic and political institutions can accommodate.

Under these circumstances, the old opposition between the "movement" and the "goal," which underlay the dual development of the world labor movement in the course of the twentieth century, no longer makes any sense to the protagonists of the struggles. As Marx had theorized, the simple exercise of the social power that has accumulated or is accumulating in the hands of labor is in and by itself a revolutionary act. An increasing number of proletarian struggles since 1968 has demonstrated the incipient recomposition of "movement" and "goal."

The recomposition was presaged and explicitly advocated in the slogan *praticare l'obbiettivo* ("putting the objective into practice") coined by

Italian workers at the height of the struggles of the late 1960s. Under this slogan, various practices of direct action were carried out. Even though practices of direct action were nothing new, their socially revolutionary effects were. The social power deployed in and through these struggles imposed a major restructuring of economic and non-Marxist working-class organizations, to accommodate the democratic and egalitarian thrust of the movement (cf. Regalia et al. 1978).

More compelling evidence of an incipient recomposition of "movement" and "goal" has come from Spain in the 1970s and from South Africa and Poland in the 1980s. In Spain, a persistent and long-drawn-out movement of proletarian struggles, which the Franco dictatorship could neither repress nor accommodate, was the single most important factor in the demise of that dictatorship and the subsequent rise of social democracy. In less clear-cut fashion, the same pattern can be identified in the later crises of dictatorships in Brazil, Argentina, and South Korea. It can also be recognized in the on-going struggles of the proletariat in South Africa and Poland. In these two cases, however, the labor movement presents specificities which enhance their significance.

The special significance of the labor movement in Poland is that it is emblematic of the contradictions and current crisis of historical Marxism as ideology and organization of the proletariat. The movement is based primarily, if not exclusively, on the social power that has been put in the hands of labor by the strategy of coercive industrialization pursued by Marxist organizations. The deployment of this social power in the pursuit of livelihood and basic civil rights is as inherently subversive of existing political and economic relations in Poland as it is or has been in all the other countries mentioned above. No distinction between the goal of social revolution and the actual unfolding of the movement is necessary or indeed possible, as witnessed, among other things, by the kind of leadership and organization which the movement has generated.

The irony of the situation is that, in struggling against a Marxist organization, knowingly or unknowingly, *Solidarnosc* has followed Marx's prescriptions for revolutionary vanguards more closely than any Marxist organization ever did. It has restrained itself (1) from forming a political party opposed to existing working-class parties; (2) from developing interests of its own separate from those of the world proletariat; and (3) from setting up sectarian principles by which to shape and mold the proletarian movement. Moreover, as advocated by Marx, its function has been more moral than political, though its political implications have been truly revolutionary.

The fact that a Marxist organization is the counterpart of this most Marxian of proletarian organizations should not surprise us in light of the foregoing analysis. As a matter of fact, the *Solidarnosc* experience provides vivid evidence in support of the two main theses of this chapter: the thesis that Marx's predictions and prescriptions are becoming increasingly relevant for the present and the future of the world labor movement; and the thesis that historical Marxism has developed in a direction that in key respects is antithetical to the one foreseen and advocated by Marx. But by bringing to the fore the role of religion and nationality in the formation of a distinctive but collective proletarian identity, the *Solidarnosc* experience does more than that. Together with the experience of other contemporary proletarian struggles, the South African experience in the first place, it warns us against excessive reliance on the Marxian scheme in charting the future of the labor movement. For in one major respect the Marxian scheme itself remains seriously defective, that is to say, in the way in which it deals with the role of age, sex, race, nationality, religion, and other natural and historical specificities in shaping the social identity of the world proletariat. The division of responsibilities among the co-authors of this book has placed all such matters beyond the scope of this chapter. But their importance for the future of the world labor movement forces me to mention them by way of qualification and conclusion of what has been said so far.

The recent experience of the world labor movement is clearly at odds with the passages from the *Manifesto* quoted in the first section of this chapter that project a withering away of the distinctive social validity for the proletariat of differences of age, sex, and nationality (see pp. 57–58 above). To be sure, the cost-cutting race of the last fifteen to twenty years has provided new and compelling evidence in support of the observation that *for capital* all the members of the proletariat are instruments of labor, more or less expensive to use according to their age, sex, color, nationality, religion, and so on. However, it has also shown that one cannot infer, as Marx does, from this predisposition of capital a predisposition of labor to relinquish natural and historical differences as means of affirming, individually and collectively, a distinctive social identity.

Whenever faced with the predisposition of capital to treat labor as an undifferentiated mass with no individuality other than a differential capability to augment the value of capital, proletarians have rebelled. Almost invariably they have seized upon or created anew whatever combination of distinctive traits (age, sex, color, and assorted geohistorical specificities) they could use to impose on capital some kind of special treatment. As a consequence, patriarchalism, racism, and national-chauvinism have been integral to the making of the world labor movement along both of its twentieth-century trajectories, and live on in one form or another in most proletarian ideologies and organizations.

As always, the undoing of these practices, and of the ideologies and organizations in which they have been institutionalized, can only be the result of the struggles of those who are oppressed by them. The social power which the on-going cost-cutting race is putting in the hands of traditionally weak segments of the world proletariat is but a prelude to these struggles. To the extent that these struggles will succeed, the stage will be set for the socialist transformation of the world.

Notes

I am indebted to Terence K. Hopkins and Beverly J. Silver for comments and criticisms on earlier drafts of this chapter.

1. In this definition of the proletariat, which I shall adopt throughout this chapter, there is no indication that workers must be engaged in particular occupations (such as "blue collar" occupations) in order to qualify as members of the proletariat. Even expressions such as "industrial proletariat" must be understood to designate that segment of the proletariat which is normally employed by capitalist enterprises engaged in production and distribution, regardless of the kind of work performed or of the branch of activity in which such enterprises operate. Marx's definition of the proletariat, however, is ambiguous concerning its upper and lower boundaries. At the upper end of the proletariat we face the problem of how to classify workers who do sell their labor power for a wage or salary but do so from a position of individual strength that enables them to demand and obtain rewards for effort that, other things being equal, are higher than those received by the average capitalist. This is most clearly the case of the upper echelons of management but it is also the case of a great variety of individuals (so-called professionals) who work for a wage or salary but are not proletarianized in any meaningful (i.e., substantive) sense of the word. In what follows all such individuals are implicitly excluded from the ranks of the proletariat unless they are explicitly referred to as being only formally proletarianized.

At the lower end of the proletariat we face the opposite problem of how to classify workers who do not find a buyer for their labor power (which they would be more than willing to sell at the prevailing rates) and therefore engage in non-wage activities that bring rewards for effort that, other things being equal, are lower than those received by the average wage worker. This is indeed the case of most members of what Marx calls the Industrial Reserve Army. As a matter of fact, the entire Reserve Army is in this condition except for the small minority of individuals who qualify for unemployment benefits or can otherwise afford to

remain fully and truely unemployed for any length of time. In what follows, all non-wage workers in the above condition will be implicitly included in the proletariat—in its Reserve Army, to be sure, but in the proletariat nonetheless.
2. All the statements of fact concerning labor unrest contained in this chapter are based on research conducted by the World Labor Research Working Group of the Fernand Braudel Center, State University of New York at Binghamton. The main findings of the research will be published in a special issue of *Review* in 1992.
3. As this sentence implies, I use the term "hegemony" in the Gramscian sense of a domination exercised through a combination of coercion and consent (Gramsci 1971: 57–58).
4. A more exhaustive account of what follows in this section can be found in Arrighi and Silver 1984.

References Cited

Abendroth, Wolfgang. 1973. *A Short History of the European Working Class.* New York: Monthly Review Press.
Aglietta, Michel. 1979. *A Theory of Capitalist Regulation: The U.S. Experience.* London: New Left Books.
Arrighi, Giovanni and Beverly Silver. 1984. "Labor Movements and Capital Migration: The United States and Western Europe in World Historical Perspective." In C. Bergquist, ed., *Labor in the Capitalist World-Economy.* Beverly Hills, CA: Sage.
Bernstein, Eduard. 1961. *Evolutionary Socialism.* New York: Schocken.
Braverman, Harry. 1974. *Labor and Monopoly Capital: The Degradation of Work in the Twentieth Century.* New York: Monthly Review Press.
Chandler, Alfred D. Jr. 1977. *The Visible Hand: The Managerial Revolution in American Business.* Cambridge, MA: Belknap Press.
Gramsci, Antonio. 1971. *Selections from the Prison Notebooks.* New York: International Publishers.
Marx, Karl and Friedrich Engels. 1967. *The Communist Manifesto.* Harmondsworth: Penguin.
Ozawa, Terutomo. 1979. *Multinationalism, Japanese Style: The Political Economy of Outward Dependency.* Princeton, NJ: Princeton University Press.
Regalia, Ida, Marino Regini, and Emilio Reyneri. 1978. "Labor Conflicts and Industrial Relations in Italy." In C. Crouch and A. Pizzorno, eds., *The Resurgence of Class Conflict in Western Europe since 1968.* Vol. I. New York: Holmes & Meier.

THE SOCIAL MOVEMENTS IN THE PERIPHERY: AN END TO NATIONAL LIBERATION?

Samir Amin

The general economic growth of the quarter of a century that followed World War II not surprisingly created many illusions. In the West, people thought that they had found in Keynesianism the definitive solution to the problem of crises and unemployment. It was thus thought that the world had entered into an era of perpetual prosperity and definitive mastery of the business cycle. In the socialist world, it was also thought that the model formula for even higher growth had been discovered which enabled Khrushchev to announce victoriously that by 1980 the USSR would have overtaken the United States "in every domain." In the third world of Africa and Asia, the national liberation movements which had seized political independence, also had a battery of prescriptions which, in a mix of capitalist and socialist recipes, in doses that varied from case to case, would enable these movements to overcome "underdevelopment" in "interdependence."

For a century or more we had become accustomed to particular forms of organization of the various currents running through society, being in the logic of a certain political praxis. In the developed capitalist societies this organization was articulated on two main themes. The first, the theme of class struggle, justified the organization of the industrial working class (trade unions, labor, Socialist and Communist parties), the model of which had sometimes inspired other popular classes (peasant or agrarian parties and unions, small business groups, etc.). The second, the theme of political ideology, justified the contrast between conservative right and reformist left. The Communist regimes came out of this history, whose forms they retained, even though, gradually, the party-state monopoly putting an official end to the "class struggle" and changes through the ballot box had distorted its meaning.

In Africa and Asia, the history of the past century had been that of the polarization of the social movement around the struggle for national independence. Here the model was that of the unifying party, setting itself the objective of bringing together social classes and various communities in a vast movement that was disciplined (often behind more or less charismatic leaders) and effective in its action toward a single goal. The regimes that emerged after independence became broadly stuck in this heritage, the single-party state deriving its legitimacy solely from the achievement of the goal of national independence.

These practices had been rationalized by what might look like a scientific theory of society. The ideology of the Enlightenment largely provided the mix of values (the humanist values of liberty, the value of welfare) and "scientific" theories underpinning their effectiveness (competition between individuals controlling the economy). The movement of socialism (including Marxism), held onto the values of the Enlightenment and, simultaneously, denounced the hypocrisy of the bourgeois content of the societal project that they purveyed, calling for it to be transcended—through reform or revolution—focusing their struggle on the class struggle. The national liberation movements themselves drew inspiration from both in varying mixtures depending on the objectives of the ruling class—or stratum—of the movement.

In the end an "equals" sign had been put between these practices and the idea of political rationality *tout court*. People forgot that the social movement had expressed itself in other ways in earlier periods, in Europe and elsewhere, among others through religions. It was forgotten that even in the apparently stabilized European West, the fragility of that rationality failed to stand up to a violent social crisis: the crisis of the 1930s had rallied vast numbers of people behind the "irrational" standards of racism and murderous madness.

Today, in the three parts of the world—West, East, and South—the models of managing social life embedded in these organizational forms seem to have exhausted their historical effectiveness.

In the West, the consensus is so broad that it has reduced the historical impact of the socialist movement and the right-left polarization, which is manifested in a sort of "depoliticization," that is, of abandonment of the ideological concern for a different global societal project. In the East, civil society aspires to break the straitjacket of the party state, in order to open up a space for the dialectic of the real contradictions running through society. In the third world legitimacy based on recovered independence is well and truly surpassed in the spirit of the younger generation.

In any event, it is striking that the discourses of power use the past tense. In these conditions, should we be surprised that the expression of unsatisfied social needs organizes itself in other ways? These new forms have already appeared: feminist movements, ecological movements, local (town and district) defense movements, ethnic or religious communal movements.

Will the future that the development of the new (or renewed when they build on old heritages) forms of expression has in store for us make possible an advance for humanity or on the contrary will it be the manifestation of a new collapse into barbarism?

Andre Malraux, with his well-known intelligence and pessimism, said that the twenty-first century would be the century of religions, meaning thereby not that of a revival of tolerant faith but that of violent conflicts of fanaticism.

But what is this system against which, or within which, the old and new social forces operate?

Is there any hesitation in dubbing it capitalist in the West and the third world? It certainly is and down to the present day has failed to transcend the limits of "actually existing capitalism as a world-system," that is, that it has not overcome the polarization between centers and peripheries. It is thus a system which continues to be unbearable for the popular masses of the third world, with or without "development." For for them it represents the poverty of the shantytowns, the frustrations of being unable to consume in a society where consumption is the norm, cultural breakdown, the arrogance of corrupt dictatorships, and sometimes even simply famine. But in the West itself, despite the social calm procured by capitalism in its advanced centers, the malaise creates an awareness of the limits of the system's capacities. In the countries of the East, I feel it is inaccurate to describe the system as capitalism too, even though it corresponds but little to the image of socialism that the Marxism which is its inspiration had portrayed. There the real social forces aspire to something different, in the confusion of the conflict between aspirations, some socialist and some capitalist, often doubtless mixed up together.

1. *Actually Existing Capitalism*

There are two ways of looking at the dominant social reality of our world (capitalism). The first stresses the fundamental relationship which defines the capitalist mode of production at its most abstract level, and, from there, focuses on the allegedly fundamental class struggle between the proletariat, in the narrowest sense of the term, and the bourgeoisie. The second stresses the other dimension of capitalist reality, its unequal development worldwide, and hence focuses its analysis on the consequences that that polarization involves at every level, thus defining other issues in the political and social struggles that occupy the front of the historical stage. Here I opt for this second way of seeing what I as a result call "actually existing capitalism."

Since the analysis suggested is predicated on the world level, the various social classes that constitute globalized capitalist society have their place in this framework, even though, in other respects, they belong also of course in the logic of the various national formations. By treating the world system as the dominant unit of analysis, we take the true measure of a social fact whose impact is decisive for an understanding of the issues in the social struggles, that is, that the bulk of the Reserve Army of capital is located geographically in the peripheries of the system. This Reserve Army is made up of course of what has become an enormous mass of urban unemployed and semiemployed (many times the number of jobless in the West even in times of crisis), but also of large segments of the mass of unwaged workers, doomed, in line with advances in these areas of activity, to be driven off their land or from the urban so-called informal activities that they are engaged in. The integration of fractions of this Reserve Army into the Active Army—always very partial—is done either on the spot through the "semi-industrialization" that characterizes the true peripheries now and in future, or by international migration to the centers. But this migration is always limited, among other things by the centers' employment strategies, and at best affects only a tiny number of the World Reserve Army.

"Liberalism" has never managed to complete its program of liberalizing trade and capital flows by unlimited opening up to the migration of workers, and thus remains truncated. This reality dominates the scene of social struggles. Doubtless at the highest level of abstraction, challenging the capitalist mode of production means eliminating private ownership of capital, along with liberation from commodity alienation and social control by workers of the whole organization of production and social life. Nevertheless, at the level of reality the revolt of the "victim" peoples of the expansion of real capitalism occupies front stage. The concept of "people" is here that of the historical bloc of the oppressed, made up of both distinctly constituted classes and the Reserve Army we have been discussing.

It is possible to recognize, in the long wave, periods that are more particularly marked by the functioning of an "integrated world market" and periods marked by the break-up of that market. Giovanni Arrighi suggests a very convincing picture of this in this volume. I add only that these successive break-ups of the unity of the world-system are the fruit, not of chance, but of necessity. For the unity at issue has never involved homogenization but the deepening of polarization precisely as a result of the always truncated character of liberalism which constitutes its ideological legitimation. It is thus perfectly intolerable for the peripheries and as a result is always being called into question. These challenges litter all actual history with violent happenings, even in periods when the unity of the system predominates, and are articulated at certain times into a set of "storms" which account for the period of global break-up of the system.

Consequently, "antisystemic" forces and movements are those that call into question this inequality, refuse to submit to its consequences, and on this ground embark on a battle which is, as a result, objectively anticapitalist, because it attacks that immanent feature of capitalist expansion that is the most strongly socially rejected.

Such a challenging of the capitalist order from revolts in its periphery obliges us to rethink seriously the question of the "socialist transition" to the abolition of classes. However many nuances are made, the Marxist tradition remains handicapped by the initial theoretical vision of "workers revolutions" opening up, on the basis of advanced productive forces, a transition which is itself relatively "rapid." This transition is moreover seen as being marked by democratic rule by the popular masses which, while it is still described as "dictatorship over the bourgeoisie" (through the means of a proletarian state of a new type rapidly beginning to "wither away"), is still considerably more democratic than the most democratic of bourgeois states. Nevertheless, all the revolutions of our time (Russia, China, Vietnam, Cuba, Yugoslavia, etc.) that are unmistakably described as socialist (and which, in the intention of their actors did indeed set themselves this goal) are in reality complex anticapitalist revolutions because they have been made in backward regions. As a result, they have not opened the era of "socialist construction" that meets the criteria initially developed by Marxism.

In the same way, and for the same reason, the attempts to "move forward" initiated here and there in the capitalist third world based on the radicalization of the national liberation movements unfailingly describe themselves as "socialist." For the same reason, the changes brought about in those places, varying in scale and intensity, and more or less fragile, scarcely meet the classic criteria of socialism.

In these conditions, real history requires that we analyze the nature and perspective of the social issues "beyond capitalism" initiated from the anticapitalist revolution in the peripheries and the radicalization of national liberation. To do so, it is necessary to go beyond ideological discourse, whether of legitimation (depending on the discourse, these are indeed socialist societies whose achievements are globally positive, despite errors . . . which are human) or of polemics (according to this discourse, these are "deviations" from a theoretical socialist model that people have in their heads and is assumed to be possible). And once ideological discourse is rejected, there remain two possible theses.

The most common thesis today is that these revolutions have in fact opened up an era of capitalist development pure and simple (and hence have in no way opened up an evolution beyond capitalism), even if it is in conflict (temporary) with the dominant centers of world capitalism, and has, as is always the case, some specific features. According to this thesis, in the last analysis, the prior passage through a phase of capitalist accumulation is inevitable. Is this not simply seeing only one aspect of the problem? For on the one hand, the bourgeois revolution is not in its deepest nature the product of a movement of the popular masses organized and led by political parties overtly anticapitalist in their ideologies and vision of the future. On the other, capitalist expansion was and continues to be globalized; that is, it involves local developments open to the world-system. Accepted by the local bourgeoisie broadly defined, this type of subordinate development is challenged by the popular masses whom it is crushing in the periphery.

The other thesis, mine, is built around the observation that the unequal development immanent in capitalist expansion has placed on the agenda of history another type of revolution, that of the *peoples* of the periphery. This revolution is *anticapitalist* in the sense that it is against actually existing capitalist development, which is intolerable for these peoples. But that does not mean that these anticapitalist revolutions are simply socialist. By the force of circumstance, they have a complex nature. The expression of their specific and new contradictions, which had not been imagined in the classical perspective of the socialist transition as conceived by Marx, gives postcapitalist regimes their real content, which is that of a *popular national construction* in which the three tendencies of socialism, capitalism, and statism combine and conflict.*

I have therefore suggested calling "popular national" the postcapitalist

---

*We are not dealing here with the problems of national popular construction (so-called socialism) in the East (see Amin 1990).

societies we are discussing which are engaged in a long historical phase whose task is essentially to erase the heritage of unequal development (knowing that that cannot be obtained by playing the game of adjustment within the world system, but on the contrary by deciding to delink). I have also suggested abandoning the ideological label "socialist societies" (they are not) or even "societies engaged in the construction of socialism." The problems which the capitalist third world countries are facing following their political liberation are not different in nature. Except that the ambiguity of strategies is here even more marked as a result of the fact that, even in the case of radicalization of the independence struggle, the option in favor of a popular content and delinking is handicapped by the bourgeois aspirations and the illusions of the project that they nurture. Why then has the third world not—or not yet—embarked on this path, the path of the construction of a popular national state?

Why does the third world assiduously try to construct a bourgeois national state in imitation of that of central capitalism? Of course, this situation is not the product of "ideas" without any social base; it is the expression of certain social classes and strata with a bourgeois vocation, which dominated the national liberation movements (i.e., the revolt against the effects of the unequal development of capitalism) and still dominate the states that emerged from it. History teaches that the bourgeoisies in the periphery have attempted this construction at every stage of world-capitalist expansion, naturally in forms appropriate to their time. Just as it teaches that in the last analysis these attempts have always been frustrated by the combination of external aggression and the internal limits peculiar to those attempts themselves.

So new popular national revolutions are among the objective requirements in the contemporary third world. Doubtless these revolutions to come will be no more socialist than the previous ones, but only popular national. No doubt too they will have their own new specificities determined by both internal conditions and external factors. These popular national revolutions will in turn modify future North-South relations and will in future constitute, as they have for seventy years, the fundamental dynamic element in the global evolution of our planet. What is at stake then in these struggles that occupy the front of the stage of modern history can thus be summed up in the alternative: popular national power (state) or compradorized power (state).

2. National Liberation and Socialism: The Old Paradigm

A certain type of Marxist and quasi-Marxist popularization introduced into ordinary political language the terms "bourgeois revolution" and "socialist revolution" as indicators of the qualitative changes that inaugurate successively the capitalist stage and the socialist stage in the development of society. This preliminary observation, trite as it might appear—too simplified to the taste of expert analysts—derives its importance from the fact that the predominant organized social and political forces in the periphery of the world-system have defined themselves precisely in relation to these "objectives," one set proposing to make the bourgeois revolution and the other the socialist revolution, each conceived as *the* effective means to achieve a "modernization," the condition of both national and social liberation.

The social dimension is here either reduced to the abolition of "backward" forms of exploitation (generally called "feudal"), or extended to all forms of exploitation—feudal and capitalist. Telescoping objectives by going beyond the bourgeois revolution and continuing the revolution to its socialist end is then deemed an objective necessity, imposed by the domination of capital worldwide and a historical possibility. Such is the core of the old paradigm on which so-called socialist and so-called national liberation revolutions have been built.

This paradigm must today be called into question in order to discover the true issues in social and political struggles beyond the appearances defined by the ideologies we are discussing.

1. *First of all, obviously, the very concept of a bourgeois revolution must be called into question.* The binary definition of the allegedly fundamental class struggle opposes exploited and exploiters in a given mode of production: peasants and feudal lords in one case, proletarians and capitalists in another. The bourgeois revolution would then necessarily be a peasant revolution and the socialist revolution a workers' one. But capitalism did not abolish feudal exploitation to replace it by an egalitarian peasant society (which was the aim of the peasant struggles); it built itself on the basis of a new form of exploitation, the very possibility of which the struggling peasants did not even imagine. The new capitalist society and the bourgeois class were formed partly on the fringes of or even outside feudal society (made up of feudal lords and peasants),—in the free cities— partly within the peasantry, through new differentiations (rich, kulak-type peasants, and landless peasants reduced to the status of agricultural

laborer) produced by the extension of market relations sometimes strengthened by peasant struggles. It is well known that this new capitalist society ripened slowly within the "old regimes," that is, within sociopolitical systems that had remained for the most part "feudal." The bourgeois revolution is then constituted by the political moment which marks the abolition of that old regime and the installation of a new type of organization assuring the political predominance of the economically dominant new class. The bourgeois revolution is then not the starting point but the crowning point of capitalist development.

But the coincidence between the peasant social revolution and the bourgeois political revolution existed in only one historical case, that of the French Revolution (as a result, the sole true revolution of the bourgeois stage of history). Here of course the bourgeoisie (both the urban bourgeoisie, the higher strata of which were made up of financiers and manufacturers, the lower strata of artisans, and the new agrarian bourgeoisie) was forced to ally with the revolting peasant masses. The vicissitudes of that alliance, its radical advances and its retreats, shaped the stages of the revolution itself and of subsequent developments. Elsewhere there was no analogous coincidence. Not even in England, where the radical bourgeois-peasant revolution of the mid-seventeenth century, perhaps because it came too soon (as witness its expression through religious reinterpretation, whereas the French Revolution secularized politics; the former came before the Enlightenment, the latter inherited it) aborted and made way for the not very glorious Glorious Revolution (which was not one!) at the end of the century. Not even in North America, where liberation from the colonial yoke was a political act without revolutionary social import, since it only confirmed the power of the market-based society of petty producers that had existed as such in New England from the beginning (it is significant that the American Revolution did not even raise the question of slavery). The same was true in Germany, Italy, and Japan. The general rule is then that capitalism developed without any peasant revolution even when peasant struggles contributed to this development or shaped the specific course of it. But not without an "agricultural revolution," in the sense that an agrarian bourgeoisie was formed, often made up of big landowners (ex-feudal lords) driving out the surplus rural population in order to modernize a production that was now largely marketed. In all these cases the bourgeoise invested the state, seized control of it, and transformed society from above.

Social Movements in the Periphery   105

Do these comments make it possible to give a different reading of the history of modern national liberation movements in the periphery of the system, and to have a better understanding of the true issues in the underlying social struggles?

2. *China 1911–80: the uninterrupted revolution.* There is an arresting parallel: from 1905 (the first Russian Revolution) to Deng Xiaoping and Gorbachev, by way of the Xin Hai, the Chinese Revolution of 1911, the Russian Revolution of 1917, the victory of the Chinese Revolution in 1949 and the Cultural Revolution of Maoism, two great societies in the periphery carried out the two revolutions which, with the French one, make up the trio of the only great revolutions of modern times. In both the Russian and Chinese cases, there was an uninterrupted movement from the "bourgeois" objective to the "socialist" objective; in both cases there was a radical peasant revolution; in both cases this peasant dimension nevertheless did not constitute the essential dimension of the transformation of society.

The Chinese Revolution of 1911 belongs in a long series of violent changes that have occurred in all the peripheries of the contemporary world-system. Integration into the world-system, which had entered a phase of deepening in the imperialist epoch (in the Leninist sense of the term), had considerably aggravated the degree of exploitation of the peasantry and had created a new national problem. The second half of the nineteenth century was, as a result, marked by a resurgence of peasant revolts in China, in India, in Indonesia, in the Ottoman Empire, in Latin America. Simultaneously, new "modernist" political forces appeared both within and outside the systems of power, in the new bourgeois strata, more often intellectuals than businessmen, in touch with the West.

The Chinese Revolution of 1911 differed fundamentally from the reformist movement of the Meiji epoch in Japan. This latter did not emerge from the struggle of the Japanese peasantry against feudalism. On the contrary, the political restoration of the power of the emperor united the Japanese feudal class around him. The state's option for modernization was as a result first strictly a technical matter: it was a matter of giving the army an effectiveness to match the challenge from the West, which gradually led to the creation of industries built up nationally. This process of maturation occurred gradually naturally in the ruling class, without the latter feeling any need to concede the least agrarian reform to the peasants. This was thus not a "bourgeois" revolution in the social sense of the term (a peasant revolution), but a political evolution of the ruling class which became bourgeois. As result also Japan did not import "democratic" ideas from the capitalist West, but only its technology.

There is still the question of knowing why the Chinese ruling class did not embark on a similar sort of capitalist transformation.

I have sketched a reply to this question in two parts. First stressing the difference between imperial China's complete tributary ideology from its peripheral Japanese form, in relation of course to the contrast between China's complete tributary mode and peripheral Japan's feudal mode (that is the core of my thesis of unequal development in the birth of capitalism; (see Amin 1980; Amin 1989a). Furthermore, the Chinese Revolution came precisely to crown peasant revolts that were decisive in the country's history.

Tributary imperial China had reached its apogee in the mid-seventeenth century, with a population of 150 million and a cultivated area of some 100 million hectares. It was thus a rich country and the tributary system levied from this relatively well-off and equal peasantry a significant surplus which made the country a great power. But during the two centuries that followed the population tripled, to reach the figure of 450 million by the mid-nineteenth century, whereas the cultivated area and agricultural methods remained virtually unchanged. The impoverishment of the peasantry reduced the surplus, which in turn weakened the centralized state, creating a risk of provincial breakdown. Neither the imperial ruling class nor the later bourgeoisie that emerged from the 1911 Revolution and the Kuomintang succeeded in resolving this dilemma: only the Communist government was able to begin to overcome it over the last thirty years. Furthermore, the deterioration of the situation in the nineteenth century, aggravated by imperialist aggression, fueled a gigantic uninterrupted series of peasant revolts (from the Taiping rebellion to the Communist Party's red bases in the 1930s). This historical continuity explains how it was possible for the bourgeois ideology of the early days of the revolution to be transcended by tacking onto it a modern socialist objective, capable moreover of integrating the rural communist traditions that are a feature of peasant struggles in all tributary societies. Therein lies the secret of this uninterrupted revolution.

The coincidence of the peasant revolution and the "anti-Manchu and anti-imperialist" revolution—analogous in a way to that which marked the French Revolution, which was both peasant and anti-monarchist—made 1911 a true revolution, or even more precisely the starting point for the long revolution 1911-49. It was a peasant-bourgeois revolution, which sought not only to liberate China from the external threat and make it once again a great (modernized) power, but which also set itself the goal initially of abolishing "feudal" forms (its own language) of the state and exploitation. Thus from the very beginning, the Chinese Revolution did not borrow from the West only its technology (as Japan did) but also claimed to be able to adopt as its own the modern ideas of democracy *inter alia*. However, the power that emerged from this first phase of the Chinese Revolution proved to be incapable of carrying out its program. The conditions were then present for the Communist Party to pursue the task, without any break in the successive stages of this revolution. Marxism—whose Afro-Asian vocation here stands out with great clarity—became the ideological instrument of that transfer.

Obviously, 1949 did not mark the end of this history, but only the beginning of a new and higher stage. I said above that subsequent developments showed that the goal of socialist construction, such as it had been formulated in the ideology of Chinese Marxism (and that of the Third International in general) was not possible, but that the long popular national phase on which it was embarked, and from which it will not emerge for many decades, constitutes not a stage in capitalist expansion, but the necessary form of its transcendence from the peripheries of the system. In a way then, the long Chinese Revolution is a popular national revolution in stages, uninterrupted stages, which has "succeeded," over and beyond the vicissitudes of its still incomplete development.

3. *Mexico, Turkey, Egypt: the interrupted revolution.* Other violent social upheavals have shaken the periphery, for example the Mexican Revolution of the 1910s and 1920s, the Kemalist revolution in Turkey (1919-24), and the series of Egyptian revolutions (1880, 1919, 1952). All these revolutions had to face the same problems as those to which the Chinese Revolution was a response: the impoverishment of the peasant masses—largely produced or aggravated by the periphery's insertion into the capitalist system—and national humiliation. Yet none of these revolutions was "carried through to the end" like the Chinese; and the three countries involved today belong to the compradorized periphery.

Yet the Mexican Revolution was initially a vast revolution by the peasantry against the commercial latifundia exploitation produced by capitalist expansion. But this revolution was controlled by a local bourgeoisie which harvested its fruits and established on that base a power that is just now perhaps beginning—half a century later—to be challenged, by other, mainly urban, social classes, moreover. The Institutional Revolutional Party (PRI) is in a way a sort of Kuomintang that has "succeeded," in the sense that it has succeeded in preventing more radical forces from supplanting it in power. So what did the Mexican Revolution produce in such conditions? Did it begin a central-type capitalist development? Not at all. It simply accelerated the deepening of Mexico's integration as a periphery in the world-capitalist system.

The Kemalist revolution lacked this peasant dimension. It emerged from a movement which, within the Ottoman ruling class, had set itself the objective of liberating the country from foreign domination by ridding it of the "traditional" local regime, which was decadent and ineffective (the Ottoman sultanate). From this angle it was a movement analogous to that of the Meiji era. Kemalist Turkey borrowed from the West—but what exactly? On the one hand, its technologies, not only of production, but—and even above all—of military, legal, and administrative organization (the modernization of the state is conceived in this way and secularism must be seen in this context). On the other hand, its nationalist ideology, nationalist in the very European sense of the word, through affirmation of the "Turkish"—Turanian—nation and renunciation of the multinational character of the Ottoman Empire.

It has already been mentioned that the Kemalist movement did not rest on a peasant movement, even when, during its military confrontation with imperialism, it was made up principally of an army of peasants (from Anatolia). This was because the dominance of a free small peasantry in the Turkish part of the empire (precisely, Anatolia) had fulfilled particular functions (supplying the bulk of the army), while other regions fulfilled other functions (notably that of providing the surplus) in this complex tributary formation.

In these conditions, it will come as no surprise that the Kemalist government—despite illusions it may have fired during the 1920s, 1930s, and 1940s—proved in the end to be incapable of "modernizing" the society in depth. On the contrary the small steps in the direction of an autonomous development (of a statist kind) were gradually dismantled during the 1950s and 1960s to make way for a deepened integration into the world system at a subordinate level (see Amin and Yachir 1988; Sertel 1987).

The history of Egypt from the reign of Mohamed Ali in the first half of the nineteenth century to the time of Nasser (1952–70) is one of a long series of national (anti-imperialist) attempts based on successive projects for relevant and large-scale social transformations. I have suggested analyzing this history as that of successive bourgeois attempts, the characteristics (and limits) of which are not unrelated to the nature of the external challenges (themselves defined by the stage of world development) on the one hand, and the nature of internal social conflicts on the other (Amin 1964; Amin 1978; Amin 1985a).

Mohamed Ali's attempt prefigured, half a century early, that of the Meiji era. Transformation was imposed from above, and aimed above all at modernizing the state and the army and ensuring the country's independence. It borrowed from the West its techniques, but ignored its ideas. It even went against the objective requirements of the sought-for modernization, since it endeavored to keep the embryonic commercial, artisanal, manufacturing, and agrarian bourgeoisie out of power and to marginalize the currents of progressive ideas engaged in a review of the interpretation of religion. The later attempt by Khedive Ismaïl, in the 1860s and 1870s, to insert the modernist development of Egypt into world development, simply ended in achieving the reverse: it accentuated internal social contrasts, to the point of making them explosive, and aggravated external dependence. It thus prepared the ground for the first Egyptian revolution of modern times, that of 'Urabi (1880–82), which was national but also social in its pronounced peasant base. Military defeat, and the British occupation that followed, explain why the 1919 revolution and the Wafd government that emerged from it (but which imposed itself on the monarchy between 1922 and 1952 only for short periods of successive crises) developed the national dimension more than the dimension of social transformation (thus the Wafd at no time considered an agrarian reform). It was thus not until the Nasserist revolution that this second dimension resumed its place in the dynamic of transformation. Carried out from above, but supported from below, this transformation (agrarian reform and statitization of the urban economy) took place this time in a general atmosphere which made it take on the colors of the "socialist perspective," after the illusions of capitalist development had been dissipated by 150 years of history. But, as I have pointed out, Nasser wanted to "build socialism" without it being the product of the initiative of the popular classes, as Mohamed Ali wanted to "build capitalism" without relying on the bourgeoisie. What happened subsequently is now obvious—recompradorization following Sadat's "counterrevolution."

4. *In countries that were colonies, the national liberation movement inevitably set itself a single immediate goal: recovery of national political independence.* That obviously does not mean that this movement had no social dimension (whether peasant or bourgeois) that varied in its content

depending on the period and the country. Peasant movements of antifeudal revolt are part of this history, as are aspirations by the bourgeoisies to control the local economic system.

Furthermore, other social and political forces—inspired by ideologies of radical so-called petty bourgeois nationalism or the ideology of the Marxism of the Third International—fought the aspirations of the bourgeoisie to control the movement and sometimes even seized the leadership of it from it in alliance or not with the revolting peasant masses. From the India of the bourgeois Congress Party to the Vietnam of the NLF led by a Communist party, by way of the plebian movements of the Algerian FLN or the Portuguese colonies in Africa, these combinations of divergent social aspirations are as varied as could possibly be.

The variety of the social content of the demand for national liberation in Black Africa did not exclude certain common features, the most notable manifestation of which was the persistence of collective forms of appropriation of and access to land which ruled out any appearance of the latifundia model that had become almost universal in the nineteenth century in Latin America and the Arab, Islamic, and Indian East. The forms of colonial exploitation, which I have suggested analyzing in terms of the three models of colonial trade economy, concession company economy, and reserve economy, perpetuated these precapitalist forms while adapting them to subordinate them to the logic of the exploitation of metropolitan capital, whether commercial or mining (see Amin 1970; Amin 1973; Amin 1988b). The subsequent—and late—development of an agrarian capitalism based on smallholdings remained itself limited to the regions where a series of favorable conditions came together as regards the structures of the traditional social hierarchies, rural population densities, and access to internal migrations. In turn, all these conditions together delayed the formation of a bourgeoisie capable of aspiring to embark on industrialization. The modalities of the national liberation movement are to be explained by all these historical conditionings. These accentuated the catalyzing role of the urban middle (so-called petty bourgeois) strata, in alliance with peasant rebellions when they existed, or with the embryonic commercial and agrarian bourgeoisies.

In the Arab world, the differences between the Ottoman Mashrek model relayed by British imperialism and the North African one subjected to the French project for colonization by settlement, gradually faded as a result of the rise of the "Nasserist model"—statist industrialist—taking over from the "liberal" latifundia model. In all these cases, the respective roles of the peasant revolt and the urban working and popular classes were important but always contained by a "populist" leadership, analysis of which I feel calls for a deeper look at the cultural and ideological dimension of the national liberation movement.

The early political independence won in Latin America by the latifundist oligarchies and the fact that that continent belongs in the European cultural area gave its social movements original patterns, also varying as a result of the different functions the countries of the region fulfill in the world capitalist system. However, despite these specificities, there are some striking parallels, at least for recent periods: the predominance of "populist" movements and the national capitalist project that they promoted from the crisis of the 1930s up to the 1950s, the dismantling of populism by the offensive of United States capital in the second half of the 1950s (with the Cuban Revolution in counterpoint), the deployment of Guevarrism in the 1960s and 1970s crushed by military dictatorships, and its exceptional prolongation in the form of the Sandinistas in Nicaragua, and then the disintegration of the military dictatorships in recent years.

To conclude, at the level of the three continents of the periphery as a whole, one can observe some common features which overlie the variety of concrete situations. Generally, the social movement goes through two successive phases that can be described, without oversimplifying, as a "liberal bourgeois" phase (based on the leadership of an agrarian-commercial latifundia bourgeoisie) and a "populist-statist bourgeois" phase (based on the leadership of an industrial bourgeoisie). These two revolutions attempted successively were interrupted by recompradorization.

The reasons for these failures vary and in each case have to do with particular unfavorable combinations (low autonomy of peasant and worker popular movements, confused ideologies, economic and political interventions by the West). But the failure is a general one and reflects what I have called "the failure of development" (Amin 1989b) and the old national liberation/socialism paradigm. The states and movements that are the heirs to that history are, as a result, stuck in their crisis and have even largely lost their legitimacy.

5. *After World War II: from the bourgeois national project to recompradorization.* If the nineteenth-century imperialist system had turned the countries of Asia and Africa into colonies, the national liberation movements were to impose the reconstruction of independent states following World War II. But did independence really open up the prospect of forming new bourgeois states whose capacity to advance along the paths of

capitalist development would henceforth depend mainly on their internal conditions? Two views split the forces of national liberation: there was the majority opinion of those who thought "development" possible in "interdependence" within the world economy, and there was the opinion of Communist parties who thought that leaving the capitalist camp would lead to the reconstruction with, if not behind, the USSR of a world socialist camp.

Despite these differences, the Asian and African states came together after the Bandung conference (1955) in the nonaligned movement (see Amin 1988a; 1989b). As one summit followed another in the 1960s and 1970s, nonalignment gradually evolved on the position of a "trade union for making economic demands on the North." The battle for a New International Economic Order embarked on in 1975, following the October 1973 war and the raising of oil prices, crowned this evolution, only to sound its death knell.

Neither politically, nor economically, was the West going to accept the spirit of Bandung light-heartedly. Is it just accidental that, a year later, France, Britain, and Israel attempted to overthrow Nasser through the 1956 aggression. The true hatred that the West had for the radical third world leaders of the 1960s (Nasser in Egypt, Sukarno in Indonesia, Nkrumah in Ghana, Modibo Keita in Mali, almost all overthrown at about the same time (1965–68), a period which also saw the Israeli aggression of June 1967, shows that the political vision of Bandung was not accepted by imperialist capital. It was thus a politically weakened nonaligned camp that had to face the global economic crisis after 1970–71. The West's absolute refusal to accept the proposal for a New International Economic Order shows that there was a real logic linking the political dimension and the economic dimension of the Afro-Asian attempt crystallized after Bandung.

What were the objectives of the Bandung project? Has this project simply run its course, having attained its objectives? Or else did it fail to attain them because that was objectively impossible? Of course, what may now be called the "ideology of development," which is now in a state of crisis that may well be fatal, and which experienced its high point precisely between 1955 and 1975, never had a meaning that was universally accepted. However, over and beyond the divergences, the general lines of what I have called the Bandung project can be recognized, albeit implicit and imprecise. I have no hesitation in describing it as the national bour-

Social Movements in the Periphery   113

geois project of the third world of our time. It can be defined by the following features:
(i) a determination to develop productive forces and diversify production (notably to industrialize); (ii) a determination to ensure that the national state should lead and control the process; (iii) the belief that "technical" models are "neutral" and can simply be reproduced; (iv) the belief that this process does not involve popular initiative as a starting point but simply popular support for state actions; (v) the belief that this process is not fundamentally in contradiction with participation in the international division of labor even if it involves temporary conflicts with the developed capitalist countries.

Realization of this national bourgeois project involved the hegemonic national bourgeois class, through its state, acquiring control in a number of areas, at least of the following processes: (i) control of the reproduction of the labor force, which implies a relatively complete and balanced development such that local agriculture be, *inter alia*, in a position to provide the basic ingredients of that reproduction in reasonable quantities and at reasonable prices to ensure the valorization of capital; (ii) control of national resources; (iii) control of local markets and the capacity to break through into the world market in competitive conditions; (iv) control of the financial circuits, making it possible to centralize the surplus and direct it to productive uses; (v) control of the technologies in use at the level of development of productive forces reached.

Seen from this angle, the experiences of the third world can be divided into two groups: those countries which have done not more than attempt to accelerate growth without worrying about the conditions listed above (Côte d'Ivoire, Kenya, Pakistan, Saudi Arabia, etc.—the list is long—and those countries which have attempted to meet the conditions mentioned (Nasserist Egypt, Algeria, Tanzania, India, Brazil, South Korea, etc.). As can be seen, the classification does not necessarily overlap the division between regimes anxious to realize a degree of social justice and reforms, notably agrarian reforms (like Nasserist Egypt or South Korea) and those which willingly accepted the aggravation of social inequalities (Brazil, for example). Nor does it necessarily overlap the division by attitudes to transnational capital (Brazil and Kenya both welcome this but the former tries to build it in to its own national policy, while the latter is satisfied to adjust itself to its requirements), nor even the question of political relations with East or West, whether of conflict or alliance. Correlations exist, of course, but the nuances of exact mixes in different concrete cases make each third world country a special case.

It is no longer possible today to ignore the inadequacies of these attempts, which have not stood up to the reversal of favorable conjunctures. Even before the current crisis offered the chance for a "Western offensive" that has succeeded in reversing the way things were going, these inadequacies had often already led to impasses. I am not saying in the abstract that these experiences were all bound inevitably to stop where they had reached and that consequently their "failure" was inevitable. I am saying only that, in order to go further, a true "revolution" was required, one capable of putting an end to the twin illusion as to the possibility of national development without such development being the product of a truly popular government and the possibility that some developments in that direction might have been possible here and there. They did not happen, and, as a result, the chance has gone.

The favorable conjuncture after World War II was that of an exceptional combination. Economically, the strong growth of the "North" facilitated "adjustment" in the South. Politically, peaceful coexistence plus the rise of Soviet industrial and military power (from the first Sputnik to the achievement of strategic parity in the 1960s and 1970s, combined with the decline of the old British and French colonialisms and the rise of the independence struggles in Asia and Africa gave the Soviet alliance a real effectiveness.

But successes always harbor their own illusions. That of a gradual, almost painless, evolution toward socialism was formulated clearly by the theory of a so-called noncapitalist road. Of course, that theory did not convince everyone. Maoists denounced it violently as the opium intended to drug peoples and calm explosions in the "zone of storms."

That page of history is indeed now turned. Since the early 1970s, the West's economic growth has run out of steam and given way to the current structural crisis. In the third world as a whole, the food crisis, the external debt crisis, and the impasses of imported technology have led to capitulation after capitulation before the *diktat* of transnational capital reorganized around the International Monetary Fund and World Bank and the consortia of the big Western banks. In radically oriented countries, *coups d'état* and military aggression have largely helped to put an end to ongoing experiences.

Is this just a passing conjuncture which will necessarily be followed by a new flowering of national bourgeois advances? Or is it a historical turning point which will no longer allow the continuation of the succession of attempts at national bourgeois projects which have marked at least a century of our history that is today ended? This in my opinion is where the real debate concerning the nature of the challenges and options for the future lies.

My hypothesis is that the contemporary crisis marks the end of an epoch, that which for Asia, Africa, and Latin America may be called the century of the national bourgeoisies, in the sense that it was precisely marked by these successive attempts to build national bourgeoisies. To observe that these experiments have not succeeded is not new. What is new, according to this hypothesis, is the assertion that analogous attempts will not happen in future. In other words, the bourgeoisie of the third world has now finally agreed to carry out its development in the compradorized subordination that the expansion of transnational capitalism imposes on it.

6. *The revolt against peripheralization which the expansion of actually existing capitalism engenders and reproduces necessarily defines the true issues of the principal social struggles in our world.* But the history of that revolt, the way in which it understood these issues, the strategy that it developed to respond to the challenge, and the results obtained stand as a warning to this 'social movement' and today ask it new questions. I would summarize the lessons of this history in the following propositions:

First: the revolt against peripheralization cannot claim to be able to resolve its problem by what I have no hesitation in calling a double impossibility, that of a bourgeois revolution and that of a socialist revolution. What it can lead to at best is a popular national revolution that is anticapitalist (because it gets out of the immanent logic of actually existing capitalism).

Second: from this viewpoint, experience—of enormous variety, there being as many cases as there are countries—illustrates only the fact that some peoples effectively managed, through an uninterrupted series of revolts and revolutions, to reach a stage of popular national revolution sufficiently advanced in the sense that the chances of moving further forward are considerable. These peoples' movement is thus the principal determinant of the evolution of the world-system toward a transcending of capitalism in its double dimension, pushing into the background (very gradually) the effects of the world polarization peculiar to capitalism on the one hand, and encouraging (equally not without contradiction) the social forces that aspire to abolish capitalist exploitation on the other.

Third: the peoples who, in this process, have been stopped in their movement at a less advanced stage are each time implacably reduced again to the subordinate status involved by the compradorization of their ruling classes. This compradorization naturally assumes the forms imposed by the global development of the system: yesterday this was principally agrarian and commercial; it is today in a determinant way industrial and statist compradorization.

Fourth: the global evolution of the system has reached a qualitatively new stage of world integration, in the sense that the margin of autonomy that hitherto permitted local bourgeoisies to "aspire" to make their "bourgeois" revolution" has disappeared. With the end of illusions of a capitalist development in stages "in global interdependence," the "century of the bourgeoisies of the periphery" is ended. Simultaneously, this deepened interdependence relinks—potentially—the movement to challenge capitalism (even if this challenge is only partial) in the centers of the system with that which engenders the permanent revolt against peripheralization. If this relinking occurs, it will make possible an evolution toward a polycentric world, a new form and a new stage in the transcending of capitalism, to which we shall return below. If it does not the dilemma remains: popular national delinking or compradorization.

Fifth: the failures of the interrupted revolution do not admit of a generalized explanation. Concrete analysis of each specific case, always irreplaceable, would probably indicate that these causes of the failure are multiple and differ from case to case: in one the absence of a peasant movement, in another external intervention, and so on. But in any event this analysis calls into question the instruments we use to understand the functioning of the ideological and cultural factor. For example, in the case of Mexico, did not the fact that the ruling classes and society belonged to European culture and their subsequent aspiration to copy the West in fact strengthen the power of the bourgeoisie and maintain its illusions? In the case of Egypt, beyond the West's precocious awareness of the "danger" that this country's renaissance implied, and, as a result, beyond the repeated military interventions (1840, 1882, permanent Israeli interventions), did not the dominance of an ideology that had remained at the tributary stage (the abortion so far of the reinterpretation of religion) share some of the responsibility?

Sixth: all the movements in the periphery have combined two main dimensions in the expression of their revolt: a national dimension and a social dimension whose content was more or less radical depending on the circumstances. Conversely, the democratic dimension, either in the narrow sense of bourgeois freedoms or in the broader sense of the autonomy of popular expression, was cruelly lacking. Once again the reasons for this are many: insufficient maturity of the local bourgeoisie, precapitalist modes of thought still dominant, immediate social concerns predominant in the popular classes, and so on. If today the political system and forces which set themselves in the popular national perspective are "in crisis" and seem to have exhausted their historical potential, it is precisely as a result of that.

Seventh: the impasses mentioned in the previous point created the conditions—very short-lived—for an imperialist counteroffensive based on a neoliberal fraud according to which without the "market" (understood as subordination to the worldwide capitalist market) there can be no democracy. It is a fraud in the sense that the generalized market (theoretically making possible, according to liberal doctrine itself, generalized development capable of overcoming world polarization) would imply the free movement of workers worldwide along with that of capital, technology, goods, and services! Truncated neoliberalism—which will necessarily be so as a result of the fact that free movement between countries is unthinkable for the foreseeable future—can thus only reproduce and deepen world polarization. As a result, compradorization renders illusory any pretention to democratization in the periphery of the capitalist system.

Eighth: the principal task of the social movement in the periphery of the system today is to impose the missing democratic dimension, not to substitute it for the national and social dimensions, but to strengthen them. In this framework the monolithic and unilateral forms of organization of the past (the party form among others) are truly being called into question. The politicization of the masses in the elevated and cultural sense of the term, involves new forms of action and organization which are perhaps now coming into being.

3. *New Stage of Transnationalization: New Issues of the Popular National Revolution*

1. *The challenge of globalization.* The above considerations have led us to suggest that the challenge of globalization has now reached a qualitatively new stage of its development. The exhaustion of the old national liberation movements (and of the most radical version of the attendant paradigm concerning the socialist transcendence of national liberation), that of the ideology of development (the Bandung era), the new forms of

financial, technological, cultural, and military transnationalization define new issues and impose on the popular social movements new objectives and new methods.

According to some, the world transformations occurring currently are such that the polarization between centers and peripheries, and the predominant form of the bourgeois national state, are on the way out, and are being replaced by a new form of globalized capitalism. In sum, it is claimed: (i) that there is no break between centers and peripheries; history is said to prove that marginalized countries can gradually lift themselves up to a higher stage of development, on condition that they insert themselves intelligently into the world-system; (ii) that the semiperipheries constitute the illusion of that possibility of which the examples of Brazil, South Korea, India, and a few others are the most recent; (iii) that the theory of dependency is linked to the agricultural or mining specialization of the countries of the periphery which is now a thing of the past; (iv) that failure to be inserted into the international division of labor leads to regression, of which the "fourth world" shows the reality; (v) that the idea that anyone can reject this insertion in order to develop outside the system (delinking) is fallacious, as proved by the nationalist attempts of the countries of the third world that have sought to accelerate their development through recipes such as "industrializing industry" and "the state as privileged actor" and whose failure is patent; (vi) that the socialist countries themselves today recognize that the continuation of their development requires their insertion into the world-system (see Amin 1985b; Amin 1987a, b, c; 1989a).

In these conditions globalization is seen as constituting an absolute, inescapable constraint. Societies that have claimed to "break" with globalized capitalism (in order to "build socialism") are said to have failed in their ambitions and to be constrained today to return to capitalism (to the "market") and want to "relink." The disillusionment produced by these "actually existing socialisms" is said to be expressed by the emergence of new social movements which no longer set themselves the traditional objective of national liberation and socialism, but are in fact more radical because they reject what most profoundly characterizes capitalism, economistic-commodity alienation, even if this rejection is limited to some particular aspect of the social totality (the status of women, ecological destruction, the nuclear threat, the critique of alienated labor, etc.). The future is said to belong to these movements, But these societies in the East and South are seen as still being caught up in old problems, largely overcome in the West (democracy, economic efficiency and the market, the satisfaction of basic needs). They thus still react badly to the true challenges of the future and, at best, carry on traditional-type partial combats (like the struggle for democracy), when they do not get bogged down in the impasse of mythological responses (like the culturalist nationalism of rejection). On the other hand, the new anticapitalist vanguard movements are growing in the developed capitalist countries, which thus reaffirm their motive role in history.

I think that all these theses are profoundly mistaken and I shall summarize my criticisms succinctly in five points:

First point: I have written elsewhere, "all quiet on the Western front." A lapidary phase which needs to be spelled out and explained, if we are to avoid misunderstandings. For quite obviously, the West is the center of numerous developments that are decisive for the global future of the world. It is the center that impels the development of productive forces worldwide, the inventor of new technologies. It is also, in some aspects of social life, the place where the most advanced breakthroughs occur. What I mean by the phrase is that the stability of Western society is such that the relations of production change and adjust to the requirements of the development of productive forces without occasioning serious political upheavals.

Let us take an actual current example. Fordism as a form of capitalist relations of production corresponded to a given stage in the development of productive forces (mass production, assembly-line work, mass consumption, the welfare state, etc.). Fordism is today in crisis: labor productivity can no longer increase on this basis, the new technologies call for other forms of organizing work, and so on. Nevertheless, everything suggests that this crisis of Fordist labor will not lead to any revolutionary political upheavals. For the West's stability rests on a double consensus: on the one hand, the acceptance by all social classes and political forces of right and left of the rules of the economic game which define capitalism (private property, the market, etc.), and on the other hand, acceptance of the rules of the political game of electoral pluralist democracy, which functions precisely because a consensus exists which does not call capitalism into question. But this double consensus is, in my view, altogether inseparable from the dominant position of the developed capitalist centers in the world-system. It is even the product of it.

Second point: It is no more true today than it was yesterday that one can "develop" within the world-system, if by that one means being capable of "catching up" and building a society based on the Western model. Naturally, capitalist expansion in the third world in the years 1945–70 was unequal. In that sense, to say that because the third world is not homogeneous, it does not exist, is neither to discover something new—for it had never been uniform, nor to answer the question, which is to know whether, over and beyond its heterogeneity, it goes through successive stages that lead it to become "analogous" to the centers of the system.

The development in question of the "semi-industrialized" countries has itself almost always aggravated and not attenuated social contrasts, thus making the terms of the alternative even sharper: compradorization or popular national revolution breaking with insertion into capitalist globalization and the international class alliances that underpin it. Is not the Brazilian example, to which we shall return when we come to discuss the topic of democracy, striking demonstration of this? Will the popular and democratic forces succeed in reversing the trend toward internal social polarization produced by the globalized capitalist "new industrialization"? But in that case, would they not precisely be beginning the transcending of the bourgeois national state by a popular national evolution? Would not the popular national state inevitably come into conflict with the West, notably over the debt produced precisely by the globalization of development? Moreover, very generally, the neopopulism of present-day Latin America (post-military dictatorships) has entered a crisis as soon as it came into being, for that fundamental reason.

Furthermore, the best results of peripheral development have not necessarily been in proportion to the degree of subordination to the imperatives of globalization; indeed quite the contrary. Here India provides an enlightening example on this point. For the relationship that India has maintained down to the present with the world-system has been relatively less constraining than that which characterizes Latin America. In fact Jawaharlal Nehru and Indira Gandhi's option was for a "semi-delinking," not only through strict controls on external trade, and transfers of capital and technology on which it was based, but in a deeper sense. Thus for example, the internal structures of the prices of staple foodstuffs and industrial prices had been semi-delinked from world structures, as has often been observed (and this delinking was the object of strong criticism by the World Bank). Gandhi's ideology and the will to isolate—relatively— Indian elites from Western models obviously played not insignificant roles in this choice. If the results obtained in the development of India are relatively honorable, they are due precisely to this semi-delinking, and not to the opposite, the opening to the outside world!

It remains the case that the contradiction of the system lies in the social content of power, largely that of a bourgeois alliance (state bureaucracy, industrial and agrarian capitalists). But these forces have always exercised pressure in the direction of reducing the "delinked" dimension of development strategies. It seems indeed that in the last few years the waning of the power of the Indian Congress Party in crisis combined with the personality of Rajiv Gandhi has encouraged the comprador aspirations of the middle classes, thirsting for immediate enjoyment. Will India as a result of this face a serious crisis? Everything suggests so. In East Asia, and particularly in South Korea, whose development has been spectacular, participation in the world economy has not been synonymous with "uncontrolled opening"; quite the contrary, the state has been omnipresent here and its intervention—at the opposite extreme from the discourse of the World Bank—decisive.

Are these latter experiences the exception that makes it possible to believe that the crystallization of new centers is still possible? It is obvious that the forms of development in East Asia (South Korea, Taiwan, Hong Kong, and Singapore) have had particular characteristics which strongly distinguish them. First, these developments, particularly in Korea and Taiwan, have been based on major agrarian reforms (certainly from fear of contagion by the Communist model) strengthened by the exceptional more egalitarian sense of Confucian ideology. Whereas in Latin America, in the Arab countries, and in South Asia, the internal market has been extended by a relative raising of the incomes of the middle strata at the expense of the popular masses, here, very unusually, wages as a whole (including those of the middle strata) have been kept at the minimum level, making possible high savings, largely public saving, while peasant incomes were substantially raised. In the Chinese states of Taiwan, Hong Kong, and Singapore, close collaboration was established with what can be called the external Chinese bourgeoisie, reaching out all over the western Pacific and Southeast Asia. In terms of population, Confucian Asia has achieved modest growth rates which reflect greater social control, and a greater penetration of the ideology of individual and family enrichment. Finally, the efforts in technical education have been much more systematic and effective. Operating on the basis of a strong national reality, these developments make the emergence of a hegemonic national bourgeoisie which appeared legitimated by quite a broad social consensus much closer, though the democratic explosion in South Korea in recent years throws some doubt on that alleged consensus.

The political analysis of semiperipheries, far then from generally disconfirming the thesis that the popular national option remains an objective necessity, reinforces its impact. If they do not make this choice, the countries in question are not in the process of "catching up," but are the true peripheries of the world-capitalist-system of today and tomorrow. For the polarization between centers and peripheries cannot be reduced to its archaic historical form (industrial countries/agricultural and mining countries), which has been or is being transcended.

As for the lamentable state of the world's poorest countries, often called the "fourth world," it is not the product of a refusal to insert itself into the international division of labor and a "failure" of a delinking attempted there. For the fourth world is not something new. The global expansion of capitalism, in its process of polarization, has always led to the exclusion of peripheral regions that have lost the functions that they had fulfilled—sometimes brilliantly—at an earlier stage. Today, the system that confines Africa to specializing in agriculture and mining based upon the extensive exploitation of its land to exhaustion, along with the technological revolution which saves on certain raw materials, are already excluding the continent from the international division of labor. Passively suffering a delinking that rejects them by definition, the societies of the fourth world cannot find an answer to their problem simply by opening up. Recolonization, sweetened by charity, aims here at masking the certain failure of the neoliberal solution.

Third point: Is it true that the countries of the East are embarked on the path of a reintegration into the world capitalist system? The argument most commonly advanced in favor of this thesis is to say that Gorbachev and Deng Xiaoping themselves talk the language of "relinking." Does that prove that their countries' social formations are identical to those of the capitalist world? That the political leadership in those countries has given up controlling their external relations to put them at the service of their own project? Such is indeed our definition of delinking. This is associated with a "transition"—beyond capitalism, and, in the long run, potentially toward socialism. That this transition is not that imagined either by Marx perhaps or by the Third International, or even by the ideology of the systems in question, that is, Bolshevism, Gorbachevism, Maoism, Deng's ideology, that it is not linear, that its arrival point is still far off are largely unknown, all that is another matter. After all, socialism has still to be built.

Fourth point: No one denies that transnationalization seems to have embarked on a new stage in its deepening. The power of modern communications undeniably has profound perverse effects on all the societies of the periphery. Does that mean that there is no possible answer to them? That there is no option but to accept as an inescapable constraint the alienation of the models proposed by capital through the globalized mass media? The food crisis in the third world is probably in part the product of food models produced by the West. But in part only and, in my opinion, in small part. For the most part, this crisis is the ineluctable consequence of the inability of the bourgeoisie and its state in our time to carry through a technological and social revolution in the countryside in the South. Beyond this impotence on the part of the bourgeoisie, the objective conditions exist for the third world to feed itself—and well—by its own means, thus rendering the "food weapon" brandished by the West obsolete. On condition precisely that it distances itself from proposals made by the West in this area: opening up agrofood operations to multinationals, kulakization through the pseudo "green revolution," giving up industry in favor of an alleged "priority to agriculture," and organized begging.

The discourse about the new (nuclear, biotechnological, computer, etc.) technologies is, I feel, largely a demagogic and facile discourse aimed at disorienting the peoples and notably at discouraging the peoples of the third world. We are told, "The train is already moving. If you don't catch it today, tomorrow you will count for nothing." I think that there is no truth in all that. And a people who, today, acquired mastery of current "ordinary" technologies (both agricultural and industrial) through its own popular national revolution would very soon be capable, tomorrow, of "catching up" in the new areas with which it is sought to impress it in order to paralyze it. On the other hand, without the mastery of technologies currently practiced, can one hope to leap directly to those of the future?

The growing centralization of capital has certainly led to globalization going through distinct stages, defined by particular and adapted forms: for example, the oligopolies of the national imperialisms in conflict between 1880 and 1945, the "multinational company" of the post-World War II period. Are we entering a new qualitative stage of the globalization of capital? Is international debt the sign of this new crystallization? Or is it merely an epiphenomenon accompanying the crisis of restructuring? These questions can—and must—be discussed. But nothing obliges us to accept that any "effective" strategy has to be placed in the logic of the demands of the expansion of capital.

Doubtless, contemporary military strategies have given the superpowers a new vision of geostrategy that no one can ignore. Does that mean that we have to submit to it? Or on the contrary must we and can we wage the political fight for a disengagement, that is, nonalignment, in the perspective of the reconstruction of a polycentric world?

Fifth point: But, it will be asked, why so much stress on national cohesion just when, in the West, there is a move to "transcend" that stage? Certainly there is here a crisis of the nation-state, at least in Europe. However that crisis, which is coming after centuries of nation-states being formed, has little in common with that of states subject from the very beginning to peripheralization. I shall claim that it is of little consequence to us what outcome the peoples of Europe find to their crisis (and we hope that it will be part of a socialist transition of Europe, which we do not see as an impossible "utopia"), we can not only wait for the reply to come from them.

Capitalist expansion has certainly created in the periphery more and more difficult conditions from the viewpoint of the formation of nation-states like those in the West. This observation is even the origin of our thesis that worldwide integration is a growing obstacle to development (and not a positive factor). The importation of state institutions copied from those of the West, which the local bourgeois ideology (and the dominant conventional social theories—of American functionalism among others) has advocated has demonstrated its vacuousness. For the expansion of capitalism in the periphery precisely ruins the chances of national crystallization, and accentuates the fragmentation and atomization of society. The crisis of social movements, the emergence of new forms of social grouping around basic communities (family, regional or ethnic, religious or linguistic), and the cultural crisis of our societies, testify to the effects of capitalist peripheralization. It is precisely because we are taking this fact into account that we speak of popular national revolution and not of socialist revolution.

I shall conclude my critical observations by reaffirming that "actually existing capitalism" remains very much an obstacle to advances by peoples and that there is no alternative to popular national transformation in the societies of the periphery. Simultaneously this transformation, initiated by the so-called socialist revolutions, has not exhausted the agenda of the objectives to be attained.

That being the case, it is difficult to say today whether the "new" movements that are emerging in the periphery (like those of the center indeed) are or are not capable of making progress toward a response to this objective challenge.

Some of these movements look to us like dead ends. This is the case with religious fundamentalist revivals or withdrawals into "ethnic" communities. They are symptoms of the crisis, not solutions to it, and exclusive products of disillusionment. They should lose steam as they reveal their powerlessness in the face of the real challenge. That is actually the expression of an optimism which believes that reason must prevail.

Others on the other hand can find their place in the rebuilding of a societal project which, "beyond capitalism," would resolve the contradictions that actually existing capitalism cannot transcend, by learning the lessons from the first steps made in that direction. It is thus each time, it seems, that the "new movements" (or the old ones!) take their stand not on the exclusive ground of "conquering the state," but on that of a different conception of the social power to be conquered. For the choice is not struggle for power or struggle for something else (what?), but what conception one has of the power for which one is struggling. The forms of organization built on the dominant "traditional" conception of power (power-state) are doomed to lose a good part of their legitimacy as the peoples come to appreciate the nature of this conservative state. Conversely, the forms of organizations that stress the many-sided social content of the power that has to be developed should experience growing successes. In this category, the theme of no party politics might prove fruitful. The same is true of antiauthoritarianism in Latin America, which Pablo Casanova sees as the principal credential of the "new" movements: rejection of authoritarianism, in the state, in the party, in the leadership, rejection of doctrinaire expressions in ideology. These are a reaction against the whole burdensome heritage of the historical formation of the continent, and doubtless a reaction that harbors progress. But also, and for the same basic reason, feminism in the West, through the objective it sets of attacking some at least of the roots of autocratism, proceeds from the same logic of a different conception of social power. In a way, the West is in the vanguard of new advances in the liberation of society. That these advances presuppose breakthroughs "beyond capitalism," or that they remain "cooptable" ("recuperable") by that social system constitutes a new field of questioning. It seems that, in the medium term at least, the advantages of a central capitalist position are such that the movements in question will not shake the foundation of the capitalist management of society.

The future of the new movements thus remains uncertain. That is why it cannot be ruled out that they may exhaust themselves in the present crisis.

Extrapolating the reflections set out by Andre Gunder Frank and Marta Fuentes in this volume, making explicit what is perhaps only implicit in what they write, it seems to me that the "effectiveness" of the social movement is not assessed by the same criteria in different periods. In periods of "prosperity" the movements easily adopt organized centralized forms. The reason for that is that they are functioning in a society where the rules of the game are known. They can, then, depending on the conjuncture, effectively realize some of their objectives (a wage increase, for example). Conversely, periods of structural crisis are defined by uncertainty as to the rules of the game, and questionings without the new order, emerging from new international and internal balances, having yet crystallized. Must the crisis of society not then necessarily involve that of ideologies, political practices, and hence forms of organization? But is it not precisely in these periods that new ideological forces crystallize and the outlines of new social projects appear, which, to paraphrase a famous quotation, "by seizing the imagination of the masses, become material forces"?

The arguments developed above do not signify that the terms of alternative are everything (i.e., that delinking—which is moreover itself a relative concept and not absolutely synonymous with autarky)—or nothing (i.e., recompradorization). Between the two extremes there is perhaps, but only perhaps, room for a "mutual adjustment" (and not a unilateral one) in the perspective of a polycentric world. And it is worth struggling for that possibility.

Unequal development engendered, reproduced, and endlessly deepened by capitalist expansion on the one hand, and the revolutions produced by the dramatic consequences of globalization in the periphery of the system on the other hand, have shaped a world too diverse for a single recipe ("the market") to be acceptable. Critical thought should thus concern itself with knowing what might be the alternative social alliances likely to get out of the vicious circles imposed by the market. From this angle the considerable differences between different regions of the world necessarily imply specific policies which cannot be derived simply from the rationality of the market. On top of these objective reasons there are equally legitimate differences to do with culture and the ideological and political options of the history of peoples. The real imperatives of our time thus imply the reconstruction of the world system on the basis of polycentrism. But to the conception of this system reduced to its political and strategic dimension (the five Great Powers: the United States, Europe—or Germany—the

USSR, China, and Japan), replacing the military bipolarity of the two superpowers, it is vital to put forward a system which gives the countries and regions of the third world their true place. Those countries and broad regions that can coordinate their visions must submit their mutual relations to the constraints of their internal development and not the opposite, namely, simply adjusting their internal development to the global expansion of capitalism.

Could a "mutual adjustment" replace the onesided adjustment proposed by the dominant liberal ideology? In a world threatened by the twin barbarism of an ever-worsening North-South contrast without hope for the peoples of the periphery (and that barbarism is already at work, if we see the true meaning of what amounts to the genocide of the peoples of the fourth world now underway by means of famine; as it already is at work in the rise of racism) on the one hand, and the nuclear threat on the other, the solution of mutual adjustment ought to appear the most reasonable. But it only has chances of progressing on condition that the objectives of the social movements in each of the three conventional parts of the world (West, East, and South) begin to converge, which in turn implies progress toward an at least partly universalist culture (we shall return to this topic in the discussion of the cultural dimension of the problem before us).

We should state clearly too that this polycentric world in no way implies any "weakening" of states, as advocated by the now fashionable antistatist ideology. On the contrary, an essential condition of what we propose is the strengthening of states—which in turn requires their democratization; without it capitalist globalization would inevitably impose compradorization on the weakest.

Finally, we should specify that mutual adjustment, like delinking of which it is simply a particular aspect, implies a "popular" power that is anticapitalist in the sense that it conflicts with the dominant capitalism but is riven by the numerous divergent interests (beyond their antisystemic convergence) of the various fractions that make up the people concerned. A social force is necessary to cement the popular alliance, overcome its internal conflicts, formulate the alternative popular national project, lead the popular bloc to enable it to achieve power, build the new state, and arbitrate conflicts between the capitalist, socialist, and statist tendencies that emerge in the long popular national transition. That is the proper role of the revolutionary intelligentsia, to which we shall also return.

2. *The democratic dimension.* In recent years, there has been a remarkable rise of the demand for democracy, both in the countries of the East

and those of the South. So much so that some observers have concluded from it that this demand is now replacing demands for national liberation and socialism, whose final failure is said to be consummated. The demand for democracy has indeed assumed proportions never before seen in the countries of the third world: in many countries it has already won the first place in the conscience of the middle classes and is penetrating into the popular, especially urban, strata. This phenomenon is probably new, since until then the demand for democracy had remained limited to particular segments of the urban bourgeoisie and had only been expressed there forcefully at particular moments of radicalization of the anti-imperialist struggles (the case of the Egyptian Wafd is one of the best examples of this). Furthermore, this democratic consciousness was in the strict limits of bourgeois liberalism. The key feature of the dominant tendencies of the popular and radical movements for national liberation was more its progressive social content than the democratic conviction of their militants, despite the use—sometimes ritualistic—of the term "democracy" and even despite the more advanced consciousness of some segments of the vanguard. I do not think I am caricaturing reality in saying that the old peasant-soldier of the Chinese Liberation Army was thinking, as he entered Beijing in 1949, of the agrarian reform, but was ignorant of the meaning of democracy. Today, on this level, his son, worker or student, has new aspirations. It was the same with the Egyptian peasant, even one voting for the Wafd, and no doubt for many others.

That is an important and definite advance, which I believe to be irreversible. But that progress does not in my opinion mean that the democratic conviction replaces national and social aspirations. On the contrary, the former reinforces the latter. Let us be clear: Marx's critique of bourgeois democracy, that it is formal and limited, remains, to my mnid, wholly correct. All the same, this democracy was not offered by the bourgeoisie to its people but conquered, relatively late, by workers' struggles. For the capitalist mode itself does not require democracy. The spring behind its social dynamism is located at another level, that of competition among capitalists and individuals. Moreover, capitalism separates economic and social management, governed by fundamentally undemocratic principles, from political management, governed today by the democratic principle of election. We would add that this form of democracy only functions when its social impact has been annihilated by the exploitation carried out by the dominant forces of the core powers within the world capitalist system, that is, the labor movement has renounced its own project of a classless society and accepts the rules of the capitalist game.

In the periphery this bourgeois democracy remains impossible and is scarcely more than the expression of the crisis of the despotic system normal in capitalism. Latin America, the Philippines, and perhaps before long South Korea and others provide glaring current examples on this level of the violent political contradictions afflicting a third world in crisis. It is well known that the theory of Latin American *desarollismo* had claimed in the 1950s and 1960s that "industrialization" and "modernization" (along bourgeois lines and within the context of even closer integration into the world-system) would automatically lead to an evolution toward democracy. "Dictatorship" was looked upon as a vestige of a supposedly precapitalist past. The facts have shown the error of this naive reasoning. Industrialization and modernization in the framework of this bourgeois project have only brought about the "modernization of dictatorship" and substituted an efficient and modern fascist-type violence for the old patriarchal, oligarchic systems. It was bound to be so: for this peripheral development implies, as we have seen, the aggravation of social inequalities, and not their reduction. In addition, the bourgeois project itself has failed to produce the promised results: the crisis has revealed the impossibility of the "independence" which legitimated dictatorship for some. By the same token, dictatorship itself entered into crisis. But are not the more or less democratic systems that came into being in these conditions confronted with a formidable dilemma? For there are only two choices: either the democratic political system accepts subordination to the demands of adjustment to the world system, and is thereafter incapable of effecting any major social reform, soon precipitating a crisis for democracy itself; or else popular forces, seizing the means provided by democracy, impose these reforms. The system will then enter into conflict with dominant world capitalism and inevitably move from being a bourgeois national project to being a popular national one. The dilemma of Brazil, Argentina, and the Philippines lies entirely in this conflict.

The absence of political democracy in the radical experiences of the third world has always operated in favor of capitalism, whether private or state, and caused the system to degenerate into a bureaucratic capitalism which, in the last analysis, opened the way to compradorization.

Democracy is the only means of reinforcing the chances for socialism within popular national society, of isolating internal capitalist relations of production from the influence of their compradorized insertion into the world capitalist system and of reducing their external vulnerability.

But what kind of democracy are we talking about? There is certainly no need to scorn the heritage of Western bourgeois democracy with its respect for rights and legality, freedom of expression of a diversity of opinions, the institutionalization of electoral processes and the separation of powers, the organization of countervailing powers, and so on. But there is no reason to stop there. To stop at Western democratic forms without taking into consideration the social transformations required by the anticapitalist revolt in the periphery leads us to become trapped in a travesty of bourgeois democracy which will remain alien to the people and consequently extremely vulnerable. In order to take root, democracy must from the outset inscribe itself in a perspective that transcends capitalism. In this area, as in others, the law of unequal development must operate here.

Obviously it is this prospect that imperialism finds intolerable. That is why the campaign orchestrated by the West about "democracy" stresses only certain aspects of the problem and neglects others. For example, it identifies multipartyism with democracy. No doubt the single party has more often than not become the expression of statist dominance.

In this respect, I shall claim that the topic of "Jacobin democracy," to borrow a term from the French Revolution, remains astonishingly up to date. In each of the three great revolutions of modern times (the French, the Russian and the Chinese), in the moment of their radicalization, the movement of ideas and social forces succeeded in projecting itself far in advance of the demands for "objectively historically necessary" social transformation. Thus Jacobin democracy went beyond demands for the mere installation of a bourgeois power. Although functioning in a framework defined by private property, its concern to establish a power that was really in the service of "the people" came into conflict with the straightforward bourgeois demand.

This forward projection was the beginning of a socialist consciousness that was yet to be born (as evidence Babeufism). In the same way, the USSR in the 1920s and Maoist China launched themselves into a communist vision well beyond the demands of the "popular national" reform on the agenda. Certainly, as a result, these moments of radicalization remained fragile and limited conceptualizations that were in keeping with the objective demands ended up by carrying the day. But it would be very wrong to underestimate their importance, because they are pointers in the direction that the necessary future movement must move.

"Jacobin democracy," rejuvenated by the contribution of the moments of radicalization of the socialist revolutions of our time, is in fact the democracy to which the popular classes of the contemporary third world aspire—however confusedly. It is marked off from bourgeois democracy, which ignores the dimension of the required social reforms, as it is from the sort of "populist mobilizations" that we have seen in Latin America, in the Arab world (with Nasserism), and in Africa (in the 1960s) whose contempt for democracy wore down the potential for renewal.

My proposal certainly does not seek to curry popularity! The fashion today is to devalue the moments of revolutionary radicalization in the name of "realism" and to favor themes coming from another tradition, the tradition of "local" democracy familiar in the Anglo-Saxon countries. "Decentralization," and the autonomy of a shattered and fragmented civil society are often proposed in that spirit, as possible realistic advances, richer potentially even than the alleged illusion of "statist" popular democracy. Movements that move in that direction, often tinged with religiosity, appear to me to suggest a strategy that is too heavily biased by antistatism to be really up to the real historical challenge.

There is something to take from all of them; and here a true dialogue is called for. Especially as the historical task of the democratic politicization of the popular classes remains a very long-haul task. The beginnings of action in that direction—through self-organization by the masses, self-development, and self-defense—have not got beyond the embryonic stage. We are thinking here of the experience of Thomas Sankara's Burkina Faso, and of others even more condemned by the dominant media in the West (Muammar Qaddafi, for example!). No doubt these beginnings are a long way from having settled the fundamental questions of the relationship between power and the parties of the so-called traditional radical left, its relationship to populism, the military, and so on.

I am not about quickly to substitute recipes that I am supposed to have the secret of for the necessary democratic dialogue among all the components of the social movement. I shall only suggest that if polarization imposes a different development the terms of the alternative are: either one accepts that "wealth" is the core value to be promoted or it is replaced by "welfare." How? First by going back to dear old Marx whose critique of the market (commodity alienation) far from being transcended, is rejuvenated by the rediscoveries of the contemporary movement. It is a market that is not to be regulated but eliminated, even though very gradually through the slow maturation of consciousness and praxis and not through bureaucratic prohibition.

3. *The cultural dimension.* Our age is marked everywhere—in the West, the East, and the South—by the emergence (or the resurgence) of social movements which express themselves in forms that one might have

thought had been overtaken since the French Revolution. Here and there individuals are once again putting their communal (ethnic or religious *inter alia*) identity before their consciousness as citizens or their class consciousness (see Amin 1989a: chs. 1, 2; Amin 1986).

The question posed by the emergence of culturalist movements is thus the following: Do these movements show that (so-called cultural) specificity constitutes by itself not only a given (that is obvious) but an irreducible and irrepressible determinant (among others) that shapes particular futures in the contrast of interdependence? Or are they only the passing expression of a historical deadend which can be transcended (but will not necessarily be so)?

These movements are too heterogeneous for any global judgment to be made, as their definition is more negative (everything that does not express class and citizen consciousness) than positive; and the content of their proposals is no less different at one extreme than the other (liberation theology cannot be confused with fundamentalism, on the pretext that both have to do with religion). I shall therefore suggest some thoughts about this cultural dimension of the contemporary social movement.

First: If economistic alienation defines the essential content of the ideology of capitalism, precapitalist class societies are governed by politics, which occupies directly the front of the stage and other aspects of social life (*inter alia* economic life) seems to have to subordinate themselves to it. This fetishization of power—necessary for the social reproduction of the system—in turn implies an ideology dominated by metaphysical concerns. Given that, the religions through which this concern is usually expressed are always flexible, so much so that they are capable, if the social circumstances so require, of adapting to the social, political, and cultural revolution of both capitalism and eventually, one day, of socialism.

In Europe, the cradle of capitalism, Christianity did indeed make its "bourgeois revolution" and rediscovered a place in the new ideological construction of the modern (capitalist) world.

At the present time, in some regions of the Christian third world (principally in Latin America), Christianity has perhaps begun another cultural revolution, in response to the demands of national liberation envisaged in a potentially socialist popular perspective. Liberation theology, which expresses this reinterpretation, is thus not in conflict with the popular national revolution but on the contrary a support for it.

Other "revivals" of the social expression of religion obviously do not have this impact. That is so, obviously, with ultraconservative fundamentalisms, such as exist in the Western Catholic or Protestant worlds. Associated with anti-third worldist racism, many of these currents represent only one dimension of the current reaction in the West (particularly in the United States).

Religious revivals that sometimes occupy center stage in the third world are more complex in nature. As regards the Islamic movements (which are in fact more diverse than the dominant media suggest), I have developed elsewhere analyses which have led me to the following two conclusions.

One, in the nineteenth century, the bourgeoisies of the Islamic-Arab world had initiated a reinterpretation of religion in keeping with the demands of modernization (capitalism); but the *Nahda*—such is the name of that movement which means "Renaissance"—was aborted on this level as the bourgeois evolution was aborted on the level of political and economic transformation;

Two, contemporary movements feed on the spontaneous popular revolt against the unacceptable conditions created by peripheral capitalism; they have so far however fallen short of making the demand for the double revolution by which modernization and popular enfranchisement must come together; and, as a result, their "fundamentalist" dimension feeding on a backward-looking myth, continues to express itself in a language in which the metaphysical concern remains exclusive in the whole social vision.

Second: Movements making "ethnic" demands, including national, paranational, or religious minorities, are also largely the product of the failure to build a national state in the periphery of the capitalist system. Going beyond their diversity and analyzing what I felt was the commonest cause of the emergence of this demand in Africa, I felt that I had to look for it in the behavior of the ruling classes which, in order to create a base that peripheral capitalist development prohibits them from acquiring by other means, manipulate ethnicity.

Third: The contemporary social movement has other dimensions. Some of these, moreover, have a universal angle and are evidence of the universality of the problems, reinforced by the intensification of communications. Feminism is the best example of this. That its impact is supremely progressive—whatever the circumstances—cannot de denied. Other dimensions on the other hand are more ambiguous in nature. Withdrawal into the "small community"—the family, the village, or the district—

sometimes facilitates the mobilization of potentials which cannot be mobilized in the more classic frameworks of parties or trade unions, either because these have lost their credibility (or because the ruling autocracy banned their activity!) or because of the atomistic character of peripheral society, poorly structured into fully crystallized classes. But such withdrawals may also reinforce negative attitudes toward popular national demands, like family-centeredness (particularly powerful in the Confucian world), or the illusion of being able to do without the state level in the transformation of reality. This latter type of illusion, which I call the "cantonalization" of consciousness, is common in the Anglo-Saxon culture area, of which it is the negative aspect, in counterpoint to the (positive) contribution of the democratic contribution of civil societies in this cultural area.

Fourth: The unity of the world, despite the polarization between centers and peripheries on which it is built, requires that the core dimension of any culture that wishes to build a better future based on the solution of the real problems of today be universalist. Diversity must serve the universalism that is to be built, not be contrasted with it as its polar opposite. It is true that peoples today are generally suspicious of universalist propositions. For, under cover of the Enlightenment, through Eurocentrism, they have legitimized their subjection or, under cover of socialism, Soviet praxis. Today "ecological" neoglobalism calls for the same reservations. That said, these reservations do not justify throwing the baby out with the bath water by rejecting the universalist perspective to be built. Here again, a certain eulogy of diversity, notably in the Anglo-Saxon tradition, borders on racism through the appeal it makes to the irreducibility of cultures. (Is not apartheid built on this alleged irreducibility?)

4. *The role of the intelligentsia.* Here we come to the discussion I propose of the specific role of the intelligentsia in the popular national revolution. I will straightaway say that this analysis is specific to the historical movement engendered by the attempt to escape from the dead end of peripheral capitalism. The concept of intelligentsia is peculiar and specific to the societies of peripheral capitalism. I know that, in saying that, I am not being very fashionable, the fashion now being rather to downplay the role of what used to be called the "vanguard."

The intelligentsia is not synonymous with either the "petty bourgeoisie" in general or even with "educated circles" (or with "intellectuals," and even less with "graduates"). The petty bourgeoise is a diverse and shifting amalgam of social strata engendered in all capitalist development—central or peripheral. As a class, globally, it plays no decisive political role; and the thesis that this class remains divided and vacillating, now leaning to the right, now to the left, seems to me to be fundamentally correct.

When Gramsci made his well-known comments about the "organic intellectual," he was assuming that each important class in history—be it dominant (the bourgeoisie in capitalism) or be it that which could aspire to become so (the working class)—produces by itself, collectively, its own ideology and culture, forms of organization, and practices. The organic intellectual is the catalyst of this production to which he gives adequate expression for the ideology of the class that he represents to turn itself into the dominant ideology in society. Gramsci further assumed that the working class in the capitalist centers was revolutionary, and, on the basis of that hypothesis, reflected on the conditions under which the organic intellectual of the socialist revolution (the vanguard party) emerges.

If one believes that Gramsci's hypothesis is wrong, and that the working class in the capitalist centers also accepts the basic rules of the game in the system, then one must deduce from that that the working classes are not here in a position, in the present state of things, to produce their own socialist "organic intellectuals." Of course they produce cadres who organize their struggles, but these are cadres who have given up thinking in terms of the alternative project of the classless society. There do indeed exist, in these societies, individuals who remain attached to that vision. But, as has already been said, "Western Marxism" is a Marxism of the debating chamber and the university, with no social impact. There also do indeed exist in these societies demands of a socialist nature which circulate and are expressed in various ways. But it is typical that these demands are not articulated in a global project (thus "Greens," feminists, etc. formally refuse to go beyond the their own specific demands), and thus that they do not produce the organic intellectual that Gramsci called for.

The situation in the periphery is totally different. Here the popular classes have nothing to expect from capitalist development such as it is for them. They are thus potentially anticapitalist. Nevertheless their situation does not correspond to that of the proletariat such as classical Marxism envisages it. For they make up a diverse amalgam of victims of capitalism hit hard in infinitely varied ways. These classes are not in a position to elaborate by themselves, and alone, a project for a classless society. They are capable—and prove it constantly—of "refusing" and even revolting, more generally of "resisting" (actively and passively). In these conditions, a historical space is opened up for the constitution of the social force capable of fulfilling this objectively necessary and possible function: that of the catalyst which formulates the alternative social project to capitalism, organizes the popular classes, and guides their action against capitalism. This force is, precisely, the intelligentsia.

The intelligentsia is not defined by the class origin of its members. It is defined by: (i) its anticapitalism; (ii) its openness to the universal dimension of the culture of our time and, by this means, its capacity to situate itself in this world, analyze its contradictions, understand its weak links, and so on; and (iii) its simultaneous capacity to remain in living and close communion with the popular classes, to share their history and cultural expression.

It remains to know what are the conditions favorable to the crystallization of such an intelligentsia, and what are the obstacles to it. In my opinion, this question, on which there has been too little reflection, is the fundamental question facing the progressive movement of our time, the true question that history has objectively put on the agenda. I shall not try to reply to it hurriedly here. I shall simply say what seems to me obvious at the level of the cultural conditions for such a crystallization. The refusal to accept and to grasp the universal dimension of culture which the real internationalization initiated by capitalism has already imposed (despite the contradictory character of this internationalization whose victims are the peoples in the periphery), this refusal and withdrawal into a negative culturalist nationalism (simply "anti-Western"—and often neurotic) do not constitute the possible yeast for an effective response. At the other extreme, Western-type alienation which definitively separates one from popular reality is also headed for a dead end.

I think that Marxism offers the only intellectual means that makes possible the necessary synthesis, at least potentially. That is why I have written elsewhere that Marxism had acquired an Afro-Asian vocation which is perhaps its principal vocation.

I shall put forward the idea that, in the spirit of this proposed analysis, the Bolshevik Party and the Chinese Communist Party were perfect expressions of the crystallization of a revolutionary intelligentsia which has effectively succeeded in organizing the popular classes and become its true vanguard. Perhaps, in the Russian case, being part of Europe was a favorable element, Marxism not appearing here as an imported foreign excrescence. Perhaps in China the secular (i.e., nonreligious) character of the traditional dominant ideology—Confucianism—was a lesser obstacle in the sense that it could not offer strong resistance to the cultural "import"—of Marxism in this case (moreover, in Japan an analogous culture did not reveal itself hostile to the import of capitalism). Conversely, perhaps, any totalitarian interpretation of religions that one may have (here Hinduism and Islam) constitutes a major obstacle to the necessary universalist openness, effective down to the present day at any event.

Conclusion

The progressive social movements of our time question the strategic choices of capital that dominates at the world level. These choices are not merely made with constraints posed by internationalization, but even more by the attempt to impose the single criterion of international competitivity on a market as liberalized as it can possibly be, but always in a truncated fashion—that is, liberalized for commodities and capital but not for labor. Such an outlook can only perpetuate polarization and worsen its consequences; it leads to the compradorization of peripheral states and thereby renders practically impossible any real advance in democracy.

The other choice for which these movements are objectively struggling is the construction of a differentiated polycentric world ("one planet, many systems"), one offering space for the autonomy of national-popular evolutions in the peripheries of the system, deriving from the dialectic of the struggle between capitalist and socialist forces both in the East and in the developed capitalist West. It is in this sense that these movements merit fully the designation of "antisystemic," even if, at their current level of strength, they remain weak and confused in their multiple guises.

Real progress beyond the confusions of our era will require a veritable convergence of strategies of the popular movements in the three parts of world society (West, East, and South). The system of real existing capitalism being first and foremost a system condemned to perpetuate, reproduce, and deepen world polarization, the revolt of the peoples of the periphery against the fate that had been ordained for them constitutes the central axis of the recomposition of an internationalism of the peoples.

References Cited

Amin, Samir. 1990. "The Future of Socialism." *Monthly Review.* May 1990.
———. 1989a. *Eurocentrism.* New York: Monthly Review Press.
———. 1989b. *La faillité du développement.* Paris: Harmattan. English edition:

Maldevelopment: Anatomy of a Global Failure. London: Zed Press, 1990.

———. 1988a. "Il y a trente ans Bandoung." In *L'échange inégal et la loi de la valeur*. Paris: Anthropos-Economica.

———. 1988b. *Impèrialisme et sous-développement en Afrique*. Paris: Economica.

———. 1987a. "The State and Development." *Socialism in the World* (Belgrade), no. 58.

———. 1987b. "Democracy and National Strategy in the Third World." *Third World Quarterly*. October.

———. 1987c. "Intellectuais, libertaçao e construçao do Estado." *Economia e Socialismo* (Lisbon). December.

———. 1986. "La fin de la Nahda." *Revue des Etudes Palestiniennes*, no. 19.

———. 1985a. *The Crisis of Arab Society*. Cairo.

———. 1985b. *La déconnexion*. Paris: La Découverte. English edition: *Delinking: Towards a Polycentric World*. London: Zed Press, 1990.

———. 1980. *Class and Nation: Historically and in the Present Crisis*. New York: Monthly Review Press.

———. 1978. *The Arab Nation*. London: Zed Press.

———. 1973. *Neocolonialism in West Africa*. London: Penguin.

———. 1970. *The Mahgreb in the Modern World*. London: Penguin.

———. 1964. *L'Egypte nassérienne*. Paris: Minuit.

Amin, Samir and F. Yachir. 1988. *La Méditerranée dans le système mondial*. Paris: La Découverte. Forthcoming in English by Zed Press.

Gattei, Giorgio. 1989. "Every 25 Years? Strike Waves and Long Economic Cycles." Paper presented at the international coloquium on "The Long Waves of the Economic Conjuncture—The Present State of the Debate," Brussels, January 12–24, Series 2.

Sertel, Y. 1987. *Nord-Sud, crise et immigration, le cas turc*. Paris: Publisud.

Silver, Beverly. 1989. "Class Struggle and the Kondratieff." Paper presented at the international colloquium on "The Long Waves of the Economic Conjuncture—The Present State of the Debate," Brussels, January 12–24. Forthcoming in A. Kleinknecht et al., *New Findings in Long Wave Research*. London: Macmillan, 1991.

CIVIL DEMOCRACY:
SOCIAL MOVEMENTS IN RECENT WORLD HISTORY

Andre Gunder Frank and Marta Fuentes

Introductory Summary

Liberty, Equality, and Fraternity (LEF) have long been and remain the explicit or implicit demands of most movements seeking social transformation. Today, of course, fraternity is complemented by sorority and may perhaps be replaced by Solidarity or Community; so we may here denominate it LEF/S.

For the past two centuries and more, the pursuit of LEF/S has successively and jointly centered (1) on revolutionary and (national) liberation movements to form or capture the state and manage state power in the quest for liberation/political democracy, (2) on labor movements as part of the class struggle in the quest for equality/economic democracy, and failing these, (3) on Marxist socialism in the quest for both and for fraternity/solidarity. These three struggles overshadowed the nonetheless also ever-present other social movements, which all along were also active both on their own and as "fronts" of progressive—and also not so—political, labor, and Marxist parties. Now these social movements themselves are increasing in importance, both absolutely and relative to the other three movements/parties/institutions, whose performance and promise is declining.

Each of these three historic movements of the nineteenth and twentieth centuries has however failed to deliver enough LEF/S goods. The state and its political parties have often failed to offer or guarantee liberty and political democracy. The labor movement and social democracy have failed to provide equality and economic democracy. Marxist-inspired really existing socialism, which was intended to succeed where the other two did (and supposedly could) not, often failed even more than they to guarantee liberty and equality. Moreover, this socialism did not even offer the fraternity/solidarity, which the dictatorship of the proletariat, let alone proletarian internationalism, had promised. Additionally, these first movements/then institutions also failed to offer adequate channels for people to pursue many other (especially cultural, gender, community, and individual) concerns, whose urgency or even relevance the "traditional" movements/institutions as often as not denied altogether. Therefore, these other concerns have been the *raison d'être* and motor force of "other" social movements all along. However, the increasingly perceived failure of the state/political parties, labor movements/parties, and socialism/Marxist parities, as well as people's increasing refusal to be manipulated by these, now also increasingly draws the "new" other social movements into the pursuit of these same classical LEF/S demands.

The same worldwide social movement to social movements, which is seeking to fill the breach left by the perceived failure of the classical political movements, parties, and institutions, is also responding to the failure of the market and other economic institutions to satisfy people's demands. Despite worldwide appeals to the "magic of the marketplace," not to mention planning, people everywhere are also banding together to pursue urgent demands, which are not provided or are denied outright by the market and/or planning. Thus, many social movements mobilize and organize for alternative social distribution and even production of "economic" goods and the pursuit of environmental and other "noneconomic" goods.

Often, these new social movements (appear to) offer a more hopeful alternative way to pursue LEF/S. Sometimes, the new social movements combine with but modify the more "classical" movements/institutions in the pursuit of LEF/S. In either case, these social movements are increasingly becoming important, if not the most important, vehicles for the pursuit of LEF/S and social transformation. Therefore, they also merit our increasing attention today in the light of their "old" history, which is often forgotten in the still long shadow of the more "classical" movements, parties, and institutions.

Since history is written by the victors, that of the vanquished, to adopt and adapt Sheila Rowbotham's title, is largely *Hidden from History: 300 Years of Women's Oppression and the Fight Against It*. But then, the same is equally true of the other social movements for peace, ecology, community, peasants, consciousness, or the like, whose history has been largely hidden, not only by victorious men, but also by the victors in class and national movements during their apparent dominance during the past two centuries of industrialization and state formation. Some of the history of the working class has emerged from hiding, despite continued class exploitation and oppression in bourgeois-dominated national states. As if by a conspiracy of these class and national victors including the male working class however, the history of the other social protest movements

Civil Democracy 141

has been suppressed and hidden. This suppression extends particularly to their collaborating overlap with each other and with the working-class movement, and most particularly to the ever-present participation of women and feminist demands in these other movements, including that of the working class. One—perhaps the most urgent—of the tasks of social history therefore is to (re)establish the rightful place of these "other" social movements in the historical social record and the contemporary social memory. The present is intended in part as an (all too modest) contribution to this task.

This task of historical reconstruction acquires increasing urgency today as multifold "new" social movements around the world increasingly mobilize more people than do the "old" class and some new national movements. Moreover, these contemporary social movements often inspire increasing popular confidence and enthusiasm compared to and in the face of the existing social and political institutions established by the old movements. Yet many of these "new" movements are themselves only the contemporary versions of similar protest movements in the past, which have been hidden from historical record and consciousness produced by history's victors. It is all the more important therefore, to deepen and widen the historical consciousness (or the consciousness about the historical precedents and roots of their own movements) of the participants—or at least the leaders—of contemporary and future social movements. This task of—literally—historical reconstruction has in recent years been most actively been pursued by oppressed women and (external or internal) colonial/ethnic/racial "minorities." We seek to extend it to other social protest and progressive vision movements as well.

Moreover, "new" social movements are today increasing in strength and importance, both absolutely and relative to state building, revolutionary and liberation movements, and particularly the reliance on political parties, which have been the tail side of the coin of state formation and colonialism. As state formation at home and colonialism abroad have been the primary political processes from seventeenth to the twentieth centuries, so have they also generated responses of revolutionary movements at home and revolutionary liberation movements abroad (that is at home from the point of view of the colonialized) in pursuit of LEF/S. In each case, the political object was state power, its formation or capture, tranformation or management often through political parties as the instrument to promote or guarantee LEF/S.

Today and tomorrow, state power and the political party as its instrument are less and less (perceived as) the purveyors or guarantors of LEF/S. Accordingly, all the less necessary and sufficient also is the pursuit of state power, revolution, and liberation through their supposedly instrumental political parties. All the most significant and ubiquitous, instead or at least in addition, became "new" social movements to address popular LEF/S concerns largely outside (and sometimes inside) political parties and beyond the state. Today, all around the world a myriad of non-political party social movements is mobilizing people in pursuit of LEF/S demands that transcend and mostly do not even include state power and revolution, though some also seek to influence state action on their behalf.

The "Ten Theses on Social Movements" by Fuentes and Frank (1989), some of which are reproduced or adapted below, find them mobilizing participants through a sense of morality and (in)justice, which develops social power through mobilization against deprivation and for survival and identity. Most "new" social movements are not new, even if they have some new features, particularly the more active participation of women. The strength and importance of social movements is cyclical and related to long political economic and (perhaps associated) ideological cycles. The class composition of social movements is mostly middle class in the West, popular/working class in the South, and some of each in the East. Some social movements compete or conflict with each other, while others overlap in membership or permit coalitions. Most social movements, however, seek more autonomy rather than state power; and pursuit of the latter tends to negate them as social movements. Although most social movements are more defensive than offensive and tend to be temporary, they are perhaps the most important agents of social transformation in that their praxis promotes participatory democracy in civil society (which we therefore call "civil democracy") and perhaps reinterprets "delinking" from contemporary capitalism and "transition to socialism." Since social movements create their own scripts as they go along like street theater, outside prescriptions of agendas, strategies, or tactics seem inappropriate. Nonetheless, they bear much new study in the light of their old history.

Cyclical History

Beyond the (hidden) relation of these "other" social movements to the "old" class and national movments, lies the relation of all these movements to the *cyclical* course of economic, political, and social history. The more "traditional" economic, political, and social processes and movements are the subject of substantial and increasing long-cycle research and popular consciousness. The "other" social movements hardly so. Therefore, we must be agnostic or at least remain still largely ignorant about their relations to economic or political cycles. We have widely differing views with regard to the relations between social movements and long Kondratieff cycles, for instance: Frank and Fuentes (1987) and Fuentes and Frank (1989) suggest that social movements are "more numerous and stronger" in Kondratieff B downward phases. Friberg (1987:2) also sees a historical relation "to so called Kondratieff cycles . . . protest activity being more pronounced during the downturn" and citing 1815–48, 1873–96, 1914–45, "and the economic downturn after 1970." Moreover, Goldstone (1980) suggests that the incidence of social movements' success "seems to depend heavily on the incidence of broad political and/or economic crisis in the society at large" (cited in Tarrow 1986:46).

Huber (1987), on the other hand, argues that "the social movements gain strength at the top, upper turning point and decline (stagnation) of a long wave, and to defuse to wider popular circles with the further course of the decline, with which by and by they however also again lose strength. With the transition to a new long wave, they recede into the background insofar as they have not exhausted and undone themselves—only to reappear again decades later with even greater force." For Huber, periods of dynamic economic expansion to 1815, bourgeois glitter-and-glory 1850–67/73, Belle Epoque 1890–1910, and economic wonder 1948/52–67/73 "forge reactive resistance and social and ecological problems," which then generate the cause and content of social movements.

For Tarrow (1986), however, although "cycles of protest and their implications for change . . . do not coincide with economic cycles in any way, protest movements appear to cluster in identifiable periods, and to be associated with substantial policy innovation during such periods." Similarly, Brand (1987) also finds that social movements come and go cyclically, but after comparing them with country-specific Kondratieff ups and downs concludes that "these movement waves *coincide not with long-term economic cycles* but with recurring waves of tendencies critical of modern civilization" (emphasis in original). Brand finds that in the past two centuries, the first wave of social movements he identifies coincides with the middle of the 1815–48 Kondratieff B downturn phase. The second one was at the turn of the century during the pronounced 1896–1913 Kondratieff upswing. An uncertain "cleft wave" of social movements in the 1920s and 1930s occurred during another Kondratieff B phase. Finally, the present wave of new social movements began at the 1960s upper turning point from the postwar Kondratieff upswing to the present Kondratieff B downswing. Thus, by Brand's reading, "mobilization waves are to be found in both down-swing and up-swing phases as well as at the turning-points of the K-cycles. There is clearly no systematic connection between the two." Finally, van Roon (1988) also fails to find any systematic connection between social movements and either Kondratieff economic cycles or even industrial or other structural transformation.

Thus, the question of the relation between social movements and economic or other cycles remains in doubt pending further research. However, we can begin to examine how social movements have (cyclically?) clusterd and been related among themselves. In so doing, of course, we also begin to examine and (re)establish the historical presence of these "other" social movements.

Social movements undoubtedly have a millenarian and global history. For present purposes however, we must confine their review to the past two centuries, for which we also have a better historical record. Nonetheless, even this record is very concentrated in a few Western countries, for which it is very country-specific. We will try, however, also to expand our review to other areas of the world, even especially by reviewing records of peasant movements around the world.

Following the compilations by our principal sources (Brand 1987, 1988 and Huber 1987) for the past two centuries, we may distinguish and classify "other" (non-class or national) social movements in core countries, principally the United States, United Kingdom, Germany, and France, as those by women, for peace, for ecology/against industry, for community, and for changes in consciouness. For other areas of the world, we may draw on the *Encyclopedia of World History* by Langer (1948, 1972). We shall also draw on Huizer (1972) for Latin America, Huizer (1980) for Southeast Asia, Mukherjee (1988) for India, and Wolf (1969) additionally for Russia, China, and Algeria to review peasant movements in these areas. The compilation on these "other" social movements is summarized in Tables 1 and 2, which offer a comparative overview of the incidence or timing by decades and sometimes years of occurrence and general location of these movements and their correlation or lack of it with Kondratieff up and down phases.

The first (impressionistic?) observation is that there seems to have been significant bunching or clustering of social movements. Not only did particular kinds of social movements, such as women's, peace, or ecological, take place over roughly the same historical periods in different countries; but all of these and other social movements in various countries also appear clustered during the same historical periods. Moreover, in Table 1 since 1800 we can distinguish three major and a couple of minor periods during which these social movements apparently became stronger and more numerous than in the intervening times. Whether this constitutes evidence for the existence of a cycle of social movements themselves is another question. The last column of Table 1 summarizes the peasant movements detailed in Table 2 and suggests that they too rose and fell in wavelike form around the world, but that the timing of peasant movements hardly coincides with that of other social movements, except during the early twentieth century.

The first upsurge of social movements (since 1800 though not necessarily the first if we look farther back) clusters in the 1820s, 1830s, and 1840s. In 1811–16, the British Luddites resisted the negative consequences of industrialization through a sort of ecological movement. Mennonites and Quakers founded peace societies after the Napoleonic Wars. Community movements in the United States and Great Britain and consciousness movements, such as romanticism, in Europe already begin earlier in the century, but continue toward mid-century, when they appeared as "Young" Germany, France, Italy, Ireland and similar movements. Women's, peace, and ecological movements, particularly in the United States and Britain, and the last also in Germany, predominate in the 1830s and 1840s, though women's movements in Britain and Germany also continue into the 1850s and 1860s.

Significantly, there were substantial links among these and other social movements. Thus the American women's movement, culminating in the 1848 Seneca Falls Convention and Declaration, had links to the contemporary temperance, other moral reform, and antislavery movements. Similarly, both American and, after the decline of the 1830s Chartists, the British (Mary Wollstonecraft) women's movement had links or overlapped with the Owenite and Fourier utopian socialist alternative communitarian movements. In Germany, the brief upsurge of a women's movement was related to the 1848 Revolution. In all these countries however, the following decades appear marked by a notable absence of recorded social movements, except for the continuation of the antislavery movement in the United States and the rise of peasant movements in many other parts of the world (see below).

Table 1: Social Movements in Recent History

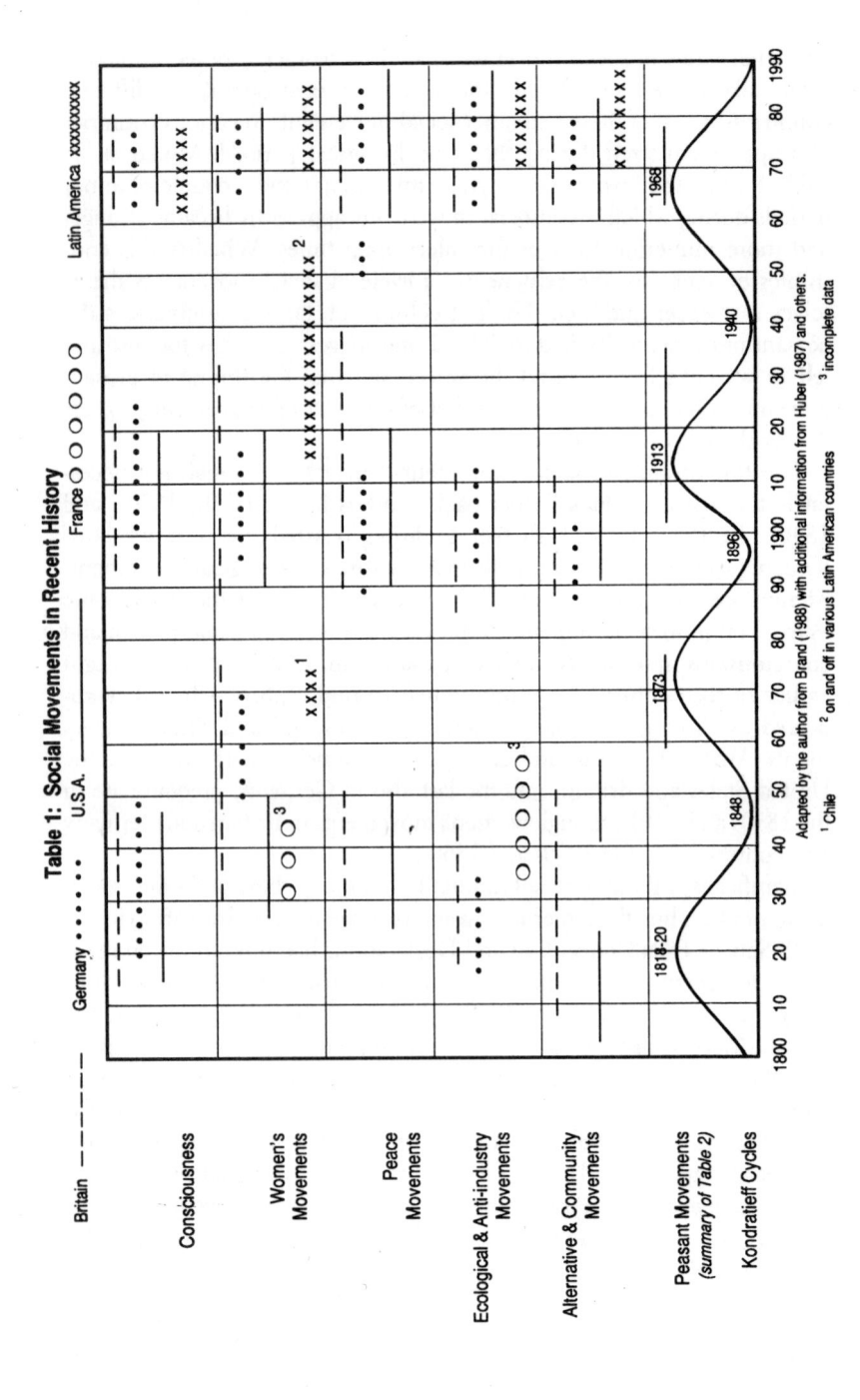

Britain — — —   Germany • • • • •   U.S.A. ———   France ○ ○ ○ ○ ○   Latin America xxxxxxxxx

Consciousness

Women's Movements

Peace Movements

Ecological & Anti-industry Movements

Alternative & Community Movements

Peasant Movements
(summary of Table 2)

Kondratieff Cycles

Adapted by the author from Brand (1988) with additional information from Huber (1987) and others.

[1] Chile   [2] on and off in various Latin American countries   [3] incomplete data

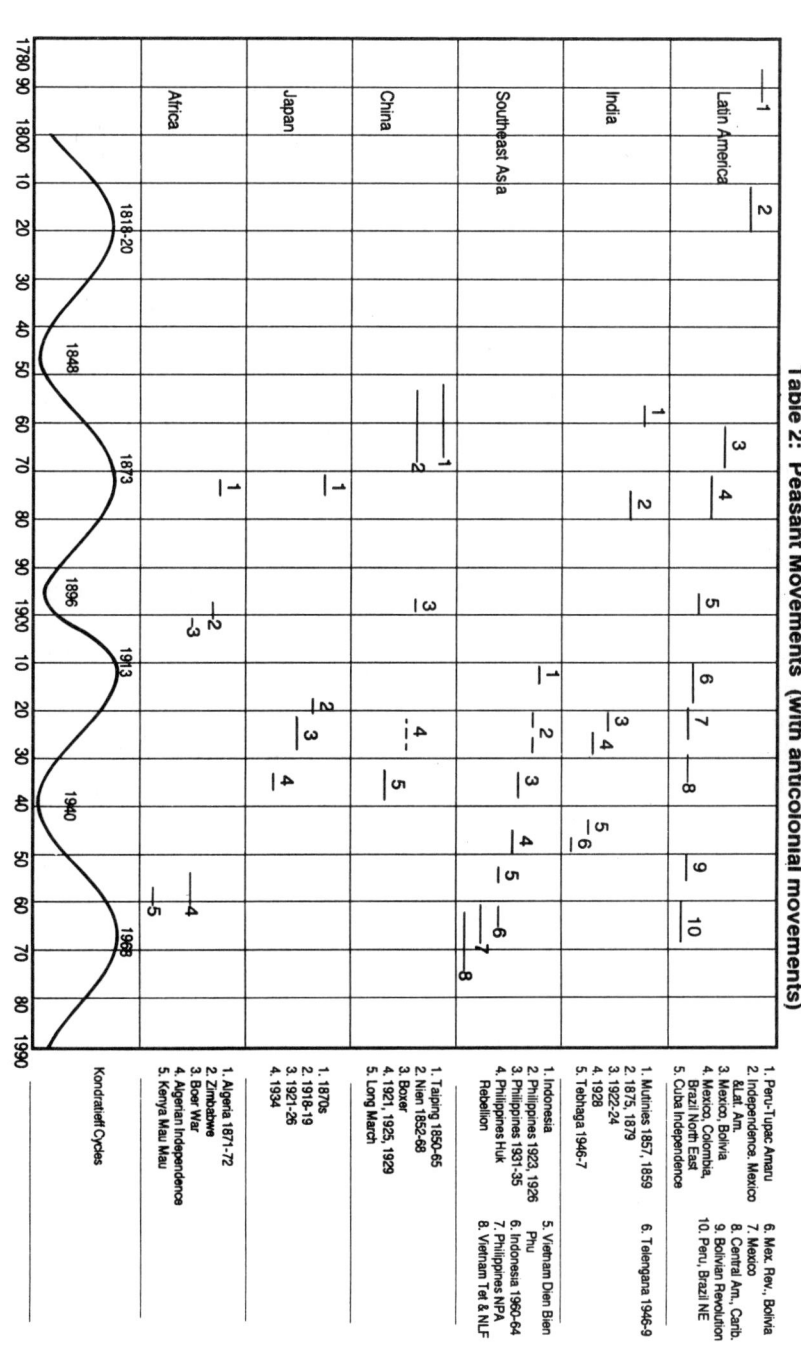

Table 2: Peasant Movements (with anticolonial movements)

Region	Events
Latin America	1. Peru-Tupac Amaru; 2. Independence, Mexico & Lat. Am.; 3. Mexico, Bolivia; 4. Mexico, Colombia, Brazil North East; 5. Cuba Independence; 6. Mex. Rev., Bolivia; 7. Mexico; 8. Central Am., Carib.; 9. Bolivian Revolution; 10. Peru, Brazil NE
India	1. Mutinies 1857, 1859; 2. 1875, 1879; 3. 1922-24; 4. 1928; 5. Telangana 1946-9; 6. Tebhaga 1946-7
Southeast Asia	1. Indonesia; 2. Philippines 1923, 1926; 3. Philippines 1931-35; 4. Philippines Huk Rebellion; 5. Vietnam Dien Bien Phu; 6. Indonesia 1960-64; 7. Philippines NPA; 8. Vietnam Tet & NLF
China	1. Taiping 1850-65; 2. Nien 1852-68; 3. Boxer; 4. 1921, 1925, 1929; 5. Long March
Japan	1. 1870s; 2. 1918-19; 3. 1921-26; 4. 1934
Africa	1. Algeria 1871-72; 2. Zimbabwe; 3. Boer War; 4. Algerian Independence; 5. Kenya Mau Mau

Kondratieff Cycles: 1818-20, 1848, 1873, 1896, 1913, 1940, 1968

The next marked upsurge, again of all of these movements and now also including peasant movements, is during the last decade of the nineteenth century and the first one of the twentieth century. The first but also the second decade of this century witness new women's movements, now everywhere demanding suffrage, in the United States, Britain, and Germany, and also in Latin America. In various countries World War I is preceded by peace, anarchist, and bohemian alternatives, as well as ecological and community movements, such as the American "wilderness cult" (conservationism, the National Park System, Sierra Club, and Audubon Society), the British "back to the country" and "garden city" movements, and the German "Heimat," and "blood and land" as well as "civilizational" consciousness movements. The 1920s and part of the 1930s witness a lesser renewed upsurge of social movements in core countries, again accompanied by peasant movements elsewhere. The latter reappear in some areas after World War II and in the 1960s. The next major cluster of bunched "new" social movements appears in the mid-1960s and continues today. Brand (1988) argues that social movements decline again in the 1980s. However, the peace and ecological movements increased in core countries at least through the mid-1980s (and Brand's table still displays them in the early 1980s), and all kinds of social movements have certainly grown in the 1980s in the socialist East and the third world South. All these movements will be the subject of our examination later in this chapter.

What sense can we make of all or even any of this? How can we relate the ups and downs of these social movements to each other, to other circumstances or cycles of economic growth, hegemony, or colonialism, and of course to the "classical" class and national movements reviewed elsewhere in this book?

First of all, the fact that other investigators not only identify but also compile and classify "other" social movements in the past is further evidence that they are not "new" but are instead a (partially hidden) part of our history. Second, the very fact that these social movements seem and tend to coincide in time from one country to another and also between different movements suggests that their upsurge(s) and abatement(s) is/are not coincidental. Apparently, they respond largely simultaneously to changing historical circumstances, which seem to occur at least part systemwide.

They may be economic. But their correlation with, let alone possible determination by, Kondratieff cycles is less than clear. The first major wave of social movements coincides largely with a Kondratieff downturn (or begins, as Huber would read it, near the Kondraftieff top). So does the current wave of social movements, which began in the late 1960s. However, the intervening second wave of social movements coincided largely with the 1896–1913/20 Belle Epoque Kondratieff upturn, and with some exceptions they weakened during the economic crisis of the late 1920s and 1930s.

Some students of social movements, like Brand (1987) and Tarrow (1983), try to account for their mobilization and especially their successes at some times and not at others on the basis of changing "political opportunity structure(s)." Tarrow analyzes and summarizes the latter in terms of changing openness and closure of social movements' political access to power, the stability or instability of political alignments within which social movements can operate, and their greater or lesser ability to find allies and mobilize support groups beyond themselves. These all sound like plausible contextual conditions to account for differential rates of social movements mobilization and success. Not unlike children's "then why that?" demands for explanations, however, this procedure only moves what is to be explained a further step back. Why then is it that in different countries and apparently circumstances these structures of political opportunity increase(d) almost simultaneously in the second quarter of the nineteenth century, at the turn of the century, and apparently again in our own time, and why did they decrease in between?

That question still remains without an answer, on economic grounds or otherwise. Tarrow only suggests as "a plausible hypothesis" that the external opportunity structure becomes more important for movement success toward the peak of the cycle. Here, however, he refers to the (peak of the) movement cycle itself, and not the (external) economic or political cycle, even though a couple of pages later he quotes Goldstone on the influence of economic and political crisis on movement success. Finally, Tarrow also observes that a favorable political opportunity structure is not sufficient for movement success. Thus, this discussion of political opportunity structure by Tarrow and others is less clear and helpful than we might wish (and in private correspondence Brand says that he does not really identify himself with it).

With regard to peasant (social) movements however, we may be on firmer ground in looking for or attributing common world-systemic changes in political-economic opportunity/necessity structures. It might seem curious to expect or find that "local" peasant movements in very different parts of the world should also share temporal clusters. And yet, although some peasant movements also appear at some other times, many important and well-known ones also seem to have occurred in bunched waves. The late 1850s to the early 1870s witnessed not only the famous Tai Ping (1850–65) and lesser known Nien (1852–68) rebellions in southern and northern China respectively, but also the well known Indian Mutiny of 1857 "which was undoubtedly the most widespread peasant revolt of the nineteenth century" (Mukherjee 1988:2115) and the 1859 Blue Mutiny or Indigo Revolt in India. However, the 1860s and 1870s also saw important peasant movements in Mexico at the time of Benito Juarez, the Brazilian Northeast, Colombia, and associated with liberal reforms in response to export agriculture elsewhere in Latin and Central America and the 1868 war in Cuba (Frank 1972), as well as in Algeria in 1871–72, and India again in 1875 and 1879.

The turn of the century witnessed a new wave of peasant movements in China, including the Boxer Rebellion, India, leading up to the revolution in Mexico, Bolivia, again war in Cuba in 1898, in Zimbabwe and the Boer War in South Africa, and in 1902 and 1905 in Russia. The 1920s and early 1930s saw important peasant movements in Japan (1921–26 following earlier ones in 1916–18), China (1921, 1925, 1930s Long March), Philippines (1923 and 1926, 1931–35/38), Vietnam, (1929), India (1922–24 and 1928), Mexico, Bolivia, Brazilian Northeast, and throughout Central America and the Caribbean (Sandino in Nicaragua, repression with 30,000 dead in El Salvador, Cuba, etc.). The decade following World War II had the Telengana Rebellion (1946–51) and Tebhaga movement (1946–47) as well as the movements related to partition in India, the Huk revolt in the Philippines, the 1952 peasant movements and revolution in Bolivia, Dien Bien Phu in Vietnam in 1954, and the beginning in 1954—after eighty years of relative quiet—of peasant and urban-based liberation movement in Algeria. The 1960s witnessed further notable peasant movements in India (Naxalite), the Philippines (NPA), the Brazilian Northeast (Ligas Camponesas), and elsewhere in Latin America.

These waves of peasant movements do, however, seem to coincide much more with Kondratieff upturn times in the 1850s and 1860s and reaching into the 1870s downturn; the early 1900s and again the 1920s and early 1930s; and the 1960s with some forerunners after wartime booms. Most students (e.g., Wolf 1968) of these movements have interpreted them as peasant reactions to commercialization of agriculture in response to growing (often foreign) market opportunities for large landowners. As the latter respond to these market opportunities, they displace their tenant and neighboring independent peasants from subsistence production on the land and thereby threaten their livelihood and security (as Frank 1967 also observed). Moreover, these peasant movements are therefore often also associated with anticolonial liberation movements. Therefore, we should not be surprised at such temporal correlations of third world peasant and liberation movements first with world-economic Kondratieff upturns, which generate the conditions for them, and then with the even sharper pain of subsequent crashes, which in turn constrain and threaten commercial agriculture and landless agricultural laborers, as after 1873 and 1930.

There may be relations between the other social movements and hegemony or peasant movements and nationalist anticolonialism. However, the fact that social movements coincide in time across countries with different and rising and falling hegemonical status also leaves their possible relations less than clear. On the other hand, the de facto relation and even alliance between some peasant and some national(ist) anticolonial and also anti-imperialist movements may be easier to establish.

To relate the "other" social movements to the "classical" labor/class and national ones examined elsewhere in this book, we may also begin by looking at their respective timing. The timing of strike waves, measured by adding up all their available data, has recently been surveyed by Gattei (1989) for five core countries using Screpanti's and other data and by Silver (1989) counting (*New York Times* and *London Times*) newspaper mentions of strikes throughout the world. Both authors found marked upsurges and peaks of strikes in the late 1840s and around 1870 (but by inference from the historical record prior to the beginning of their data series) and in their own data after 1890, around 1920 (after World War I), the late 1940s (after World War II), and Gattei but not Silver for the late 1960s. Both authors try to relate their strike peaks to Kondratieffs, and Gattei remarks that his peaks coincide with both upper and lower Kondratieff turning points. His argument that they reflect increased turning point tensions is less convincing. We must consider that some strike peaks come after wars (although Goldstein 1987 argues that these wars in turn come at Kondratieff peaks). Also strikes occur mostly locally and sectorally (even if Gattei adds them up internationally). Yet his Kondratieff dating refers to the world or at least core economy and is not necessarily matched by all local, sectoral, or national peaks and troughs, which might be reflected by strikes.

Nonetheless, we can see some temporal overlaps between their strike peaks and our "other" social movements, which we have plotted in a more rough-and-ready fashion by decades in our Table 1. Our first upsurge of "other" social movements, especially in the 1830s and 1840s, certainly coincides with the class (and also national) movements of these same decades, culminating in the revolutionary and reform movements of 1832 and 1848. The renewed upsurge of social movements at the turn of the century also begins with, but continues after, the strike peak of the early 1890s. In our own century, social movements again coincided in time, but less so in strength and extension, with the strikes after World War I, and again (if there was a strike peak) in and after the late 1960s. However, we did not find a marked upsurge of social movements other than peasant movements around 1870. Now, a century later, the labor movement is weakening (and nationalist movements are growing) during the present period of social movement upsurge.

It would be desireable to make such a comparison with possible waves of national movements, but we lack a similar plotting for them. However, we can observe roughly that national movements also increased in the 1840s, around 1870, around and of course during the world war periods and again now. So national movements seem to have rough "coincidence" with the strike and other social movements. Moreover, the peasant movements plotted in Table 2 probably contain components of both national and agricultural labor movements in the third world with some relation to both Kondratieffs (as noted above) and other movements elsewhere.

This historical review of social movements leaves unresolved—indeed unconsidered—the question of whether their more-or-less synchronized ups and downs constitute or are the result of a social movement cycle. It has been argued that there are independent cycles of ideology (Sorokin, Sarkar), American politics (Schlesinger Senior and Junior), and other aspects of social life. Brand (1988 and personal correspondence) argues that social movements reflect "discontinuous social change" in response to "cultural crises when the cultural paradigm is eroding," which is specific to and differs from one sociocultural-political unit to another. However, these "cycles'" supposed generational and other mechanisms of phase changes, recurrence, and self-perpetuation are far from satisfying the criterion of sine wave like autogeneration of a true cycle. Moreover, while these supposed ideational cycles may overlap here and there or now and then with waves of social protest movements, it would be hard to demonstrate their identity over history. Thus it would be hard to demonstrate that the ups and downs of social movements coincide with, much less have their source in, an underlying ideational cycle.

On the other hand, Andrew Jamieson argues:

> Social movements have been the source of many important social innovations in the development of science and technology, new ways to organize both the production, as well as the dissemination of knowledge. Even more important perhaps, social movements have altered the boundaries of the officially sanctioned institutions for knowledge production. By bringing new concerns into the arena of public debate, social movements have provided much of the basis for reorganization of the social institutions of knowledge production. . . . Could they perhaps even be a crucial ingredient in the eruption of Thomas Kuhn's famous—or infamous—"scientific revolutions"?. . . . Social movements can be said to have a cosmological function, acting as "social carriers" for new world-views or conceptions of man and nature. (Jamieson 1988: 72,74).

Thus, Jamieson also examines some of the abovementioned bunched conceptual and ideological developments, such as utopian socialism in the second quarter and environmentalism in the last quarter of the nineteenth century, as manifestations of their apparently cyclically arising social (movement) carriers. As to the possible existence of some independent *cyclical* mechanism of auto-generating phase change among social movements themselves, we are not aware of any serious attempt to demonstrate any and certainly cannot attempt any here.

State Formation in Nationalist and Socialist Revolution

Despite the hidden history of these other social movements, the most visible macro political process during the nineteenth and twentieth centuries centered on state unification and formation, if necessary preceded by "national" liberation from another state, and often accompanied by interstate conflict. The state was at the center of the attention and the political party the principal instrumentiality of both Ins and Outs of power. Largely replacing community and other forms of social integration, state ideology increasingly came to define citizenship, nationality, political rights (that were misnamed civil rights), and often even personal identity. In order to manage these socio-political characteristics identified with the state, the Outs sought to rely on political parties to achieve and then perhaps transform but always manage state power through revolution or reformism. Also bourgeois, petty bourgeois, labor, nationalist, and Marxist revolutionary and/or reformist class movements all relied on political party instruments to seek national state power, be it by violent and fast or peaceful and slow means. Bourgeois representatives of capital, national bourgeois representatives of national capital, socialist (sometimes more self-styled than real) representatives of labor all regarded state power and the political party as the necessary and sufficient instrument of political, economic, social, and cultural policy formation and implementation. The Outs sought to replace the Ins by revolution or reform to manage—and relying on their own political party—the same (state power) means, if not to the same (particularly economic) supposedly LEF/S ends.

The now all-too-similar conservative, liberal, and Marxist views and policies about the state and the economy are symptomatic of changing views and policies about the necessity and sufficiency of the state (and therefore revolution) and particularly political parties with regard to other LEF/S concerns as well. These changes derive from objective and subjective changes in the instrumentality of the party and the power of the state itself in the economy and the society. We may consider these changes under the headings of the external powers of the (nation) state in extra- or inter-national affairs, and in intranational powers of the state in domestic affairs.

The world economy existed prior to and always was largely beyond the control of (national) states, which were formed in important respects better to compete in the world economy. This historical fact is contrary to almost universal opinion about the supposed primacy of the (nation) state, which is reflected in the terminology of "international" trade and other relations. This common, if rather unrealistic, belief in the power of the state with regard to the (world) economy of course supported the economic interest in state power. However realistic or not in the past, present, and foreseeable future, reality increasingly undermines both the supposed fact and the perception of state power in the face of increasingly powerful world-economic forces. These are increasingly beyond the control of any state, including those of the United States and Japan, or the Soviet Union and China, and a forteriori of any European and third world state. This external economic weakness of the state—and a forteriori of any political party to run it—therefore increasingly calls into question the sufficiency and perhaps even the necessity of having, capturing by revolution or otherwise, and managing or transforming state power through political parties for economic (LEF/S?) purposes.

Individual states are also weak externally due to the "strength" of rival and other states. These limit the power and sufficiency of any one state, or even the alliance of several states, in the interstate system. Perhaps this relative weakness of states was always implicit in the interstate system, but modern technological and other, including economic, developments have further exacerbated this weakness of virtually all of the 159 members states of the United Nations. This fact of international life may not do much to inhibit revolutionary enthusiasm, but it does reduce the political chances of achieving state power through revolution against domestic *and* foreign opposition; and it certainly inhibits the exercise of any revolutionary power if once achieved.

These world realities are also reflected in the changing relationship between (Marxist) class struggle/revolution and (bourgeois) nationalist struggle/revolution, which next to war were the perhaps most important macropolitical processes during the last century. In the nineteenth century socialism and nationalism were rival and mostly mutually exclusive forces. Each considered an alliance with the other only in the supposedly rare cases in which such a tactical alliance would almost certainly further its own cause more than that of its potential ally. This conflictive relationship between nationalism and socialism changed in the twentieth century. The conflict over and competition for state power remained in the West. Indeed, they sharpened further, particularly in the fascist states, despite Mussolini's early socialism and the official National Socialist name of the Nazi party. (Fascist [social] movments then and now, whether they aspire to and/or achieve state power or not, deserve more attention than they receive here). Nationalism and socialism became mutually exclusive mortal enemies in the West, the more so the more imperial(ist), national(ist), and offensive the state was. However, the more a people or their (potential) country was subject to this imperialism or colonialism, the more did local nationalism and socialism become not only tactical but often strategic allies. This defensive alliance became widespread and almost universally accepted as "natural" throughout much of the twentieth century in the colonial and neocolonial third world and in Lenin's and Stalin's wartime Russia/Soviet Union and after the Japanese invasion in China as well.

After widespread decolonization in the third world, however, nationalism and socialism again turned to much greater rivalry. Moreover, everywhere iron nationalism proved stronger than wooden socialism. Every socialist revolution and movement had a strong nationalist component, but many nationalist ones had little or no socialist input and no or less and less socialist output. Today, in any even combat for popular allegiance or state power, nationalism wins hands down over socialism.

Ironically, this nationalist victory over socialism is especially pronounced and evident in the "socialist" countries. This nationalist and ethnic strength is now painfully evident in the multinational Soviet Union and Yugoslavia, and in the strained relations among socialist states and even more so their populations, such as with Poles and others in Eastern Europe (e.g., between Rumania and Hungary), in the Sino-Soviet split, or in the Sino-Vietnamese war and Vietnamese occupation of Cambodia.

Ironical also, however, is the surviving and often still-growing strength of nationalism, if often not national(ist) revolution, in the face of the increasing external weakness and its growing evidence in the world-economy and interstate relations, as observed above. Why make and respond to national(ist) appeals if national state power is increasingly and evidently ineffective toward the outside? The answer maybe must be sought in the usefulness and use of nationalist sentiment and ideology to maintain and increase the *internal* power of the state—against socialist as well as other movements and interests.

Paradoxically, the growing external weakness of states seems to be matched by their internal strength to defend themselves and their incumbents in power against its revolutionary usurpation, socialist or otherwise. The revolutionary capture of state power is now virtually inconceivable in the West. Much the same is true in most of the South, although in some states (palace) *coups d'état* occur with alarming frequency. However, these changes of (who is in) government rather than the state change little of essence and certainly do not promote LEF/S. Moreover, the coups seem to be more possible precisely among those states that are the most ineffectual.

The crowning irony of state formation and revolutionary transformation, however, is the increasingly demonstrated and perceived inability and insufficiency of state power and party politics to address widespread popular LEF/S concerns in civil society. Even the most democratic states, not to mention the many repressive ones, have a now demonstrated incapacity to offer or guarantee the liberty, equality, and fraternity/(sorority?)/solidarity, in whose name the French Revolution was made two centuries ago. The bourgeois political democracies in the West, where they guarantee liberty, have failed to offer or guarantee democratic economic equality. The socialist economic democracies in the East, less unequal albeit not equal, have failed to offer, much less to guarantee, democratic political liberty. The states in the South have failed on both counts of liberty and equality. Significantly, all states, West, East, and South, have failed to offer democratic fraternity, not to mention sorority, or solidarity in the multitude of relations and concerns of civil society.

Everywhere today, both in political reality and in popular perception, the state and party politics falls far—and apparently increasingly—short in addressing, let alone satisfying, popular LEF/S concerns in civil society. Despite popular mandates and official pretensions, states everywhere have failed to address or resolve problems of economic exploitation and deprivation; political oppression; peace threatening or disturbing insecurity (1987 witnessed the highest number of third-world wars ever); environmental degradation; ethnic, religious, gender, age, and class discrimination, marginalization, and injustice; regional, sectoral, and community (mal)integration or segregation; and individual and other crises of identity, which are more or less rampant everywhere. Recently, these state failures have received important political expression and official recognition, for instance through the electoral process in the United States, Britain, and France; through popular manifestations and official pronouncements in the Soviet Union, Poland, and Rumania; and through all these in China, India, and Brazil (which on May 13, 1988, celebrated in the breach the abolition of slavery a century ago). In each case state party politics has shown itself to be an insufficient instrument even to address, let alone to achieve, all sorts of LEF/S demands. Thus, revolution is proving to be transitory or transitional in three senses of the word. One is the classical transition from before to after the revolution. Another is the counterrevolutionary thermidor, which displaces the revolutionaries or even reverses the revolution itself and/or reveals that many if not most of the revolutionary LEF/S demands have not been attained. A third sense of transition is that from (the) revolution itself as disillusion spreads with the possible LEF/S results or limitations of revolution. In particular, the limitations in the possible political, economic, social, and cultural LEF/S fruits, which are apparently inherent to the state power and its exercise especially through hierarchical political parties, generate additional or alternative movements to transform society in the pursuit of LEF/S.

Therefore, we may also distinguish three senses in, or reasons for, which other sociopolitical movements represent or effect a transition from revolution and reliance on political parties to other forms of social transformation for LEF/S. One is that the limitations of revolution and state power as well as political parties as their instrumentalities generate increased popular reliance on other sociopolitical movements instead of revolution and political parties to attempt social transformation, independently of their respective rates of LEF/S success. Moreover, these other social movements express and effect popular demands for LEF/S more directly than moving indirectly by way of capturing or exercising state power through political parties to the same ends. Experience demonstrates that, contrary to the Marxist critique of "utopian" socialism, state power is *not* necessarily the necessary or even a sufficient intermediary step to promote, much less to guarantee, a whole series of social LEF/S demands. Still less so is the "Leninist" (really Stalinist) political party. Finally, the transition from revolution to social movements is socially transformatory, because the very social act of making these social LEF/S demands through social movements—the going itself, independently of the getting there—itself already represents a transformation of society in the sense of exercising civil democracy in civil society.

A *Marxist Socialist Parenthesis*

In this regard, Marxism and socialism have come full circle in praxis and theory: From (1) Marx's development of productive forces until they enter in contradiction with the relations of production, to (2) Lenin's and especially Stalin's revolutionary change of the relations of production through the capture and management of state power to permit developing the forces of production (and to proceed in little more than a decade from the first stage of communism to the second) and Khrushchev's "goulash communism" that would "bury" the capitalist United States in twenty years, to (3) Mao's changing consciousness through cultural revolution to safeguard state power and promote changing relations of production and developing forces of production, back to (4), which equals (1) the classical Marxist position on socialism. Herein, Deng Xiaoping, Mikhail Gorbachev and countless third world socialist leaders have returned full circle to the classical Marxist position about the development of the forces of production before LEF/S and above all. (The ex-revolutionary prime minister of Zimbabwe, Robert Mugabe, declared he is "not only a practicing but also a practical Marxist"). Except that now any contradictions of this development with relations of production are postponed into the unforeseeable future—and for now it is time to play economic catch as catch can. In other words, now state power may still be regarded as necessary (although not for the working class), but it certainly is no longer regarded as sufficient to develop the forces of production. On the contrary, for Marxists as for followers of Ronald Reagan, Margaret Thatcher, or Jacques Chirac, the development of the forces of production is seen to take place at the margin of state power and direction, which now often appear to be literally counterproductive.

In this regard, some recent pronouncements from China may be taken as representative of the new Marxist theory and praxis everywhere. Chinese Premier Zhao Ziyang told the Thirteenth Party Congress in 1987 that "the backwardness of the productive forces determines the following aspects of the relations of production . . . [and] all this shows that we still have a long way to go before we advance beyond the primary stage of socialism" (Quoted in Ma Ji 1988:13). Zhao Ziyang continued in the same report:

> Whatever is conducive to the growth [of the productive forces] is in keeping with the fundamental interests of the people and is therefore needed by socialism and allowed to exist. . . . To believe that it is possible to jump over the primary stage of socialism, in which productive forces are to be highly developed, is to take a utopian position on this question and is the major cognitive root of Left mistakes. (Quoted by Schram 1988)

The consensus of a meeting of more than eighty Marxist theoreticians, journalists and publishers in Bejing "was that the theory of the primary stage of socialism is the central part of Zhao's report . . . [and] should be deemed an important breakthrough in the theory of scientific socialism and a major development of Marxism. . . . As a result, our socialist theory agrees with the realities better, the significance of which is immeasurable" (Ma Ji 1988:9,12).

The same author also observes that "Deng Xiaoping once said, the basic task of socialist society is to develop the productive forces. . . . Whether it is helpful to expand the productive forces should be the point of departure in our consideration of all problems and the basic criterion for judging all our work" (Ma Ji 1988:11).

Under the title "Developing Marxist Economic Theory in the Practice of Reform," another author explains that therefore we should

> establish a new concept that the ownership structure is determined by the nature of the productive forces. . . . The criteria for embodying the superiority of socialist public ownership . . [lie in] whether the form of this type of public ownership conform to the need for the development of productive forces and whether they are beneficial to arousing laborers' enthusiasm and bringing about effectiveness in the use of resources. . . . Therefore, during the stage of modern socialism, especially during its primary stage, we can

only proceed from the actual level of social productive forces and work according to the requirements of developing social productive forces, introduce the market mechanism to develop commodity economy. . . . (Liu Guoguang 1988:25, 26, 30)

In another article on "The Economy of the Primary Stage of Socialism," the author generalizes

we should, proceeding from Marx's theory that the development of social productive forces is the fundamental task of socialism, affirm and permit the long-term existence of individual and capitalist economies in the primary stage of socialism in China. . . . Moreover, I am also of the opinion that China is not the only country which needs a primary socialist stage in its development of socialism. (Yu Guangyuan 1988:77).

Finally, the *International Herald Tribune* (June 1, 1988) reports:

In a recent article in *People's Daily*, Li Honglin, a prominent social scientist, declared flatly that socialism had failed. He said that "in the field of economy, the arena of competition is the marketplace, where the price and quality of goods make all the difference between the success and failure of the enterprises and where the customers mete out the final judgment. Since a socialist society cannot eliminate competition, the only way out is to face up to the reality and let competition work." Naturally, Mr. Li explained, in a competitive economy, some people will get rich first. "But it also stimulates the people trailing behind to catch up and narrow the gap," he said.

Thus, the problematique and prospects of transition to socialism may be reinterpreted in view of the experience with really existing socialism and contemporary social movements.

Really existing socialism has proven unable to delink from the world capitalist economy. Moreover, despite its achievement in promoting extensive growth (by mobilizing human and physical resources), it has failed to provide adequately for intensive growth through technological development. Indeed, the same state planning which was an asset for absolute industrial autarchic national growth has proven to be a liability for competitive technological development in a rapidly changing world economy. The related political organization of really existing socialism has lost its efficacy at home and its attraction abroad. Most importantly perhaps, it is becoming increasingly clear that the road to a better "socialist" future replacement of the present capitalist world-economy does not lead via really existing socialism. As the Polish planner Josef Pajestka observed at a recent meeting at the Central School of Planning and Statistics in Warsaw, really existing socialism is stuck on a side track. The world, as one of the present authors remarked, is rushing by in the express train on the main track, even though as Pajestka retorted, it may be heading for an abyss. Indeed, the utopian socialists—whom Marx condemned as utopian instead of scientific—may turn out to have been much less utopian than the supposedly scientific socialists, whose vision has turned out much more utopian than realistic. In seeking and organizing to change society in smaller, immediate but *doable* steps, which did *not* require state power, the utopian socialists were perhaps more realistic than the scientific ones—and they were more akin then to the social movements of our time than the "scientific" socialists of the intervening century. What is more, many utopian socialists proposed and pursued social changes and particularly different gender relations, which were subsequently increasingly abandoned or forgotten by scientific socialists. Marx and his scientific socialist followers thought that incorporating women more into the labor force would be both necessary and sufficient to equalize gender relations. Such incorporation of women took place massively in the really existing socialist countries, albeit perhaps more to harness their labor to extensive growth; but this economic expedient has not anywhere proven sufficient to make women equal to men.

In *Eve and the New Jerusalem*, Barbara Taylor documents the struggle, and where possible the implementation, of women's rights and of participatory democracy by the (Robert) Owenite utopian socialists, and the importance of the same as well among those associated with Fourier and Saint-Simon. Participation was also present in the early Marx as an antidote to the alienation, which concerned him and again many social movements today. Thus, some contemporary social movements might benefit from greater familiarity with the goals, organization, and experience of earlier utopian socialists—and of some anarchists as well.

The real transition to a "socialist" alternative to the present world-economy, society, and polity, therefore, may be much more in the hands of the social movements. Not only must they intervene for the sake of survival to save as many people as possible from any threatening abyss. We must also look to the social movements as the most active agents to forge new links, which can transform the world in new directions. Moreover, although some social movements are sub-national, few are national or inter-national (in the sense of being between nation states), and many like the women's, peace, and ecological movements could be trans-national (that is non-national) or people-to-people within the world-system. Not surprisingly perhaps, there is more transnationality among metropolitan-based social movements than among the more fragmented ones in the also more fragmented dependent third world. This real social(ist) transformation—if any—under the agency of the social movements will, however, be more supple and multifarious than any illusionary "socialism in one country" repeated again and again.

Autonomous Self-Empowerment and State Management

To address these LEF/S concerns themselves, in face of the external weakness of the state and its internal strength but inefficacy, people in civil society everywhere are moving to mobiize themselves through a myriad of social movements beyond or besides, and often instead of, political parties, the state, and revolution. Moreover, in the postwar era economies prospered and the rules of the game more or less worked. Social protest movements were weaker and/or more or less played by the rules of the game. However, in the course of the present world economic crisis rates of economic growth have declined or become negative. The establishment's established political (party) rules of the game have also ceased to work so well and/or increasingly fail to offer people acceptable options. Therefore, as Samir Amin has suggested, social movements now move to write their own new and different rules of the game through their praxis, according to which they wish to pursue LEF/S and seek to change society generally without relying on political parties to capture or manage state power.

Most social movements do not seek state power, but autonomy, also from the state itself. For many participants and observers, this statement is a truism. Not seeking—let alone wielding—state power is a *sine qua non* of a social movement, and state power would negate the very essence and purpose of most social movements. This incompatibility between social movement and state power is perhaps most intuitively obvious for the women's movement(s). On the other hand, for both participants and observers of social movements, it is hardly satisfactory to define or even describe them in terms of what they are not, instead of what they are. The most numerous—because individually small-scale—social movements, which are community based, of course, cannot seek state power. However, similarly to the women's movement, the very notion of state or even political party power for them would negate much of their grassroots aims and essence. These community movements mobilize and organize their members in pursuit of material and non-material ends, which they often regard as unjustly denied to them by the state and its institutions, including political parties. Among the non-material aims and methods of many local community movements is more grassroots participatory democracy and bottom-up self-determination. These are (sensed as being) denied to them by the state and its political system. Therefore, the community movements seek either to carve out greater self-determination for themselves within the state or to bypass the state altogether.

These community movements have recently mushroomed all over the South and West, although perhaps less so in the East. Of necessity, in the South the community movements are more concerned with material needs—and often survival itself—while in the West many can afford to devote greater attention to local grassroots participatory democracy. Of course, the for them uncontrollable forces of the national and world-economy severely limit the community movements' room for maneuver. Not even national states have sufficient power—and do not protect the communities—in the face of world-economic forces beyond their control. That is why—perhaps ironically since they are even more powerless—the local communities attempt protection on a self-empowering, do-it-yourself basis. Collective action and direction are consciously pursued and safeguarded, and concentration of power is shunned as corrupting (as though speaking Actonian prose).

The other side of this same coin is—especially during the economic crisis—the increasing disappointment and frustration of many people with the economy itself. "Economic growth," "economic development," "economic ends," "economic means," "economic necessities," "economic austerity"—so many economic slogans and "solutions"—and they do not satisfy people's needs for community, identity, spirituality, or often even material welfare. Moreover, political (state) institutions are perceived as handmaidens rather than alternatives or even satisfactory directors of these supposed economic imperatives. No wonder that particularly women, who suffer the most at the hands of the economy, are in the forefront of non- and antieconomic extrainstitutional social movements, which offer or seek other solutions and rewards.

Many social movements also respond to people's frustration with and sense of injustice toward political-economic forces beyond their control. Many of these economic forces—some(times) perceived, some(times) not—emanate from the world economy in crisis. Significantly, people increasingly regard the state, and its institutions, particularly political parties, as ineffective in face of these powerful forces. Either the state and its political process cannot or it will not face up to, let alone control, these economic forces. In either case, the state and its institutions as well as the political process and political parties where they exist, leave people at the mercy of forces to which they have to respond by other means—through their own social movements. Accordingly, people form or join largely protective and defensive social movements on the basis of religious, ethnic, national, race, gender, ecological, peace, as well as community and various "single" issues. Most of these movements mobilize and organize themselves independently from the state, its institutions, and political parties. They do not regard the state or its institutions, and particularly membership or militancy in political parties, as adequate or appropriate institutions for the pursuit of their aims.

Indeed, much of the membership and force of contemporary social movements is the reflection of peoples disappointment and frustration with—and their search for alternatives to—the political process, political parties, the state, and the capture of state power in the West, South, and East. The perceived failure of revolutionary as well as reformist left-wing parties and regimes in all parts of the world adequately to express people's protest and to offer viable and satisfying alternatives has been responsible for much of the popular movement to social movements. However, in many cases people's grievances are against the state and its institutions; and in some cases social movements seek to influence state action through mostly outside—much more rarely inside—pressure. Only some ethnic and nationalist, and in the Islamic world some religious, movements seek a state of their own. Should the latter be excluded from the category of "true" social movements, as one of the present authors argues?

One of the major problems of and with social movements, nonetheless, is their coexistence with national states, their political institutions, process, and parties. Despite, or indeed perhaps because of, their autonomous self-empowerment, many social movements nonetheless seek to influence or change the management and actions of the state, government, party, and other establishment institutions. Many single and also multiple issue movements seek to exercise social or political pressure on the executive or legislative power to accede to or implement movement demands. Community movements demand state services or infrastructure for their locality. Ecological movements demand state protection of the environment. Peace movements demand changes in state foreign policy. Women's movements demand legal changes.

Many social movements also have reciprocal relations with political parties, which threaten to affect their respective organizational forms and identities. The following recent instances are illustrative of the resultant problems. The upsurge of "clubs," movements, and demonstrations in the Soviet Union and Eastern Europe has many non-party elements—but often also many party members—that seek to change party procedures and state action, but without superseding them. Community movements in Argentina, Brazil, Chile, and Mexico have important mass and political inputs into—but they have not replaced—the old or even new political parties, which oppose(d) military and other institutionalized state power. In the United States, Jesse Jackson's Rainbow Coalition sought to and to some extent did change the Democratic Party. Between the 1984 and 1988 presidential campaigns, however, the Rainbow Coalition's social movement ceded much more to the party—and its labor constituency—than vice versa; and Jesse Jackson himself became a much more serious Democratic Party candidate.

Historically, moreover, many existing political parties started out as social movements; and this also means that some social movements turned into parties. In many Western countries, such as Germany and Britain particularly, Social Democratic, labor, and other progressive, as well as regional(ist), parties often started out as progressive social movements in the nineteenth century. They then turned themselves into parties, which survive in the present century. In many third world countries also, movements became parties. In India and virtually everywhere in Africa, (anti-)colonial liberation movements became political parties upon independent state formation. Asian Communist parties, as in China, Vietnam, Indonesia, were such from the beginning; but they derived their initial force from their participation in liberation movements and became bureaucratized parties thereafter.

However, also in formally already independent third world states, some political parties started out as movements. In Mexico, Bolivia, and Cuba, successively, revolutions and their movements became ossified and institutionalized, giving rise to such contradictions in terms as the Mexican PRI (Institutionalized Revolutionary Party). In Venezuela and Peru, anti-dictatorial Democratic Action (AD) and Popular Action (AP) movements became political parties after the dictatorships' downfall. In Argentina, the Peronist party started as a movement, and perhaps the Radical one also. In Chile, the now centrist Radical Party and also the Socialist Party started as progressive movements in the nineteenth and twentieth centuries, respectively. Moreover, a feminist movement became a political party with parliamentary representation in Chile. Feminist movements also turned into political parties elsewhere, as in Peru and Spain. Of course, in several countries the Moviemiento(s) de Izquierda Revolucionaria (MIR) became (Leninist) political parties while retaining their movement names.

Another illustration of this problem and sequence is the Green Movement/Party in Germany. The originally grassroots ecological movement became a political party in the parliament. The "Realo" (realist realpolitik) wing argues that the state, parliament, political parties, and so on are a fact of life, which the movement must take account of and use to its advantage, and that influence is best exerted by entering these institutions and cooperating with others from the inside. The "Fundi" (fundamentalist) wing argues that participation in state institutions and coalitions with other political parties like the Social Democrats compromises the Greens aims and prostitutes their fundamentals, including that of being a movement. Ethnic, national, religious, and some peace and community movements face similar problems.

Whatever these movements can do outside the state, the pressure sometimes becomes irresistible also to try to act within the state, as or as part of or through a political party or other state institution. But then the movement(s) run the danger of compromising their mission, demobilizing or repelling their membership, and negating themselves as movements. The question arises, whether the end justifies the means and is more achievable through other more institutionalized non-movement means. Moreover, the question arises whether old social movements which were often created as mass front organizations of political parties are now replaced by new social movements, which themselves form or join political parties. But in that case, what difference remains between the old and the new social movements, and what happens to the non/extra/anti-state and party sentiments and mobilization of many movement members? Perhaps the answer must be sought by shifting the question to the examination of the internal life-cycle of social movements or the replacement of old movements by new movements and to the aforementioned external political opportunity structure. Perhaps, to return to Samir Amin's suggestion, at more favorable times this structure offers greater opportunities successfully to press demands and reforms through political parties, labor unions, and other institutional channels within the rules of the game. At other more unsettled times the opportunity structure permits/obliges social movements to arise and to write their own extrainstitutional rules of the game. Finally, the changing political opportunity structure may again favor the greater institutionalization of some movements or their conversion into political parties and other organizations more successfully to pursue some of the same aims.

Thus, it is necessary to consider both the wider societal context and the longer historical/cyclical timeframe to evaluate the success or failure of social movements both within and against the system. The reference in this context to "antisystemic" (social) movements (for instance by Amin and Wallerstein) requires clarification, however. Many social movements are indeed *anti*systemic in the sense that the movements and their participants combat or otherwise challenge the system or some aspect thereof. However, very few social movements are anti*systemic* in their attempt, and still less in their success, to destroy the system and to replace it by another one or none at all. There is overwhelming historical evidence that social movements are *not antisystemic* in this sense. Indeed, social movements often achieve a measure of success by institutionalizing their demands or even themselves within the system. On the other hand, as we observed above, the social consequences of "pure" social movements themselves are scarcely cumulative. Moreover, their effects are often unintended, so that not infrequently these effects are incorporated if not coopted by the system, which ends up being invigorated and reenforced by social movements, which were formally anti-systemic but did not turn out to be antisystemic. There is scarce contemporary evidence that in the future the prospects for social movements and their consequences will be very different from the past. Indeed, the systemic means, ends, and consequences of social movements—even if some are subsequently coopted—are to modify the system "only" by changing its systemic linkages.

Moreover, as social movements come and grow cyclically in response to changing circumstances, so do they go again. Of course, if the demands of a particular social movement are met, it tends to lose force as its *raison d'être* disappears (or it is institutionalized and ceases to be a social movement). More usually, however, the circumstances themselves change (only in part if at all thanks to the social movement itself) and the movement loses its appeal and force through irrelevance or it is transformed (or its members move to) another movement with new demands. Moreover, movements mobilize people rather than institutionalizing action. Even when they are unsuccessful or still relevant to existing circumstances, social movements tend to lose their force as their capacity to mobilize wanes. This susceptibility to aging and death is particularly true of a social movement that is dependent on a charismatic leader to mobilize its members. The various 1968 movements and most revolutionary and peasant movements are dramatic examples of this cyclical life cycle of social movements.

Class Composition

The new social movements in the West are predominantly middle-class based. This class composition of the social movements, of course, reflects in the first instance the changing stratification of Western society from more to less bipolar forms. The relative and now often absolute reduction of the industrial labor force, like the agricultural one before it, and the growth of tertiary service-sector employment (even if much of it is low waged) and self-employment increased the relative and absolute pool of middle-class people. The decline in industrial working-class employment has reduced not only the size of this social sector but also its organizational strength, militancy, and consciousness in "classical" working-class and labor union movements. The grievances about ecology, peace, women's rights, community organization, and identity, including ethnicity and minority nationalism, seem to be felt and related to demands for justice predominantly among the middle classes (particularly in the professional educational service sectors) in the West. However, ethnic, national, and some religious movements straddle class and social strata more. In particular, minority movements, such as the black civil rights and the Latin Chicano movements in the United States, do have a substantial popular base, though much of the leadership and many of their successful demands come from the middle class. Only nationalist chauvinism and perhaps fundamentalist religiosity (but not religious cultism and spiritualism) seem to mobilize working-class and some minority people more massively than their often nonetheless middle-class leadership. Although most of these people's grievances may be largely economically based through increased deprivation or reduced or even inverted social mobility, they are mostly expressed through allegiance to social movements, which pursue feminist, ecological, peace, community, ethnic/nationalist, and ideological demands.

In the third world, social movements are predominantly popular and working class. Not only does this class/strata have more weight in the third world, but its members are much more absolutely and relatively subject to deprivation and (felt) injustice, which mobilizes them in and through social movements. Moreover, the international and national/domestic burden of the present world economic crisis falls so heavily on these already low-income people as to pose serious threats to their physical and economic survival and cultural identity. Therefore, they *must* mobilize to defend themselves—through social movements—in the absence of the availability or possibility of existing social and political institutions to defend them. These third world social movements are at once cooperative and competitive or conflictive. Among the most numerous, active, and popular of these social movements are a myriad of apparently spontaneous local rural and urban organizations/movements, which seek to defend their members' survival through cooperative consumption, distribution, and also production. Examples are soup kitchens; distributors and often producers of basic necessities, like bread; organizers, petitioners, or negotiators, and sometimes fighters for community infrastructure, like agricultural and urban land, water, electricity, transport. Recently there were over 1,500 such local community/movements in Rio de Janeiro alone; and they are increasingly widespread and active in India's 600,000 villages.

In other words, "the class struggle" in much of the third world continues and even intensifies; but it takes—or expresses itself through—many social movement forms as well as through the "classical" labor (union) vs. capital and "its" state one. These popular social movements and organizations are other instruments and expressions of people's struggle against exploitation and oppression and for survival and identity in a complex dependent society, in which these movements are attempts at and instruments of democratic self-empowerment of the people. In the third world, region, locality, residence, occupation, stratification, race, color, ethnicity, language, religion, individually and in complex combinations, are elements and instruments of domination and liberation. Social movements and the "class struggle" they express inevitably must also reflect this complex economic, political, social, cultural structure and process.

However, not unlike working-class and peasant movements before, these popular movements often have some middle-class leadership and now ironically offer some opportunities for employment and job satisfaction to otherwise unemployable middle-class and intelligentsia; professionals, teachers, priests, who offer their services as leaders, organizers, or advisers to these community and other popular third world social movements.

More often than not, these local community movements overlap with religious and ethnic movements, which lend them strength and promote the defense and assertion of people's identity. However, ethnic, national, and religious movements also straddle class membership more in the third world. Ethnic, religious, and other "communal" movements in South

Asia (Hindu, Moslem, Sikh, Tamil, Assamese, and many others) and elsewhere in the third world—and perhaps most dramatically and tragically so in Lebanon—also mobilize peoples against each other, however. The more serious the economic crisis, and the political crisis of state and party to manage it, and the greater the deception of previous aspirations and expectations, the more serious and conflictive are these communal, sometimes racial, and also community movements likely to grow in the popular demand for identity in many parts of the third world.

The (so-called) socialist East is by no means exempt from this worldwide movement to social movements. However, in the East social movements are more pluriclassist than in the West and South. The 10 million mobilized by Solidarity in Poland and various movements in China are well-known examples. More recently the Soviet Union and many parts of Eastern Europe have been increasingly visited by similar movements. In the Soviet Union, tens of thousands of "nonofficial" groups or "clubs" have sprung up under the umbrella of glasnost and perestroika to press every which kind of demands—but often on the Communist Party and the state—for which official channels have been wanting. Nationalist demands, often for economic reasons and in the Baltic republics associated with economic and ecological demands, have been mobilizing huge masses of demonstrators. Nationalist demonstrations and charismatic leaders are threatening not only again to Balkanize but now also to Africanize much of the Balkans and Central/Eastern Europe.

In short, ethnic, nationalist, religious, ecological, peace, women's, regional/community, and (other) protest movements with varied social membership are on the rise both within and outside of the institutional and political structure throughout the socialist countries because of and in response to changing circumstances, which are similar to those in the rest of the world. However, corresponding to the socialist East's intermediary or overlapping position between the industrial capitalist West and the third world South (if these categories still have any utility or meaning, which is increasingly doubtful), the social movements in the socialist East also seem to straddle or combine class/strata membership more than in the West or the South.

Coalition and Conflict

We may inquire into likely possibilities of conflict and overlap or coalitions among different (kinds of) social movements. Aristophanes already remarked on the relation between women and peace in *Lysistrata*. Riane Eisler (1987) has traced this same relation even farther back in human society in her *The Chalice and the Blade*. Today, the women's and peace movements share membership and leadership and certainly offer opportunities for coalition. Substantial participant or membership and leadership overlap can also be observed between women's movements and local community movements. At least women are especially—and in Latin America preponderantly—active in community movements, where they acquire some feminist perspectives and press their own demands, which serve to modify these movements, their communities, and, one hopes, society. In the West, there is a similar if lesser overlap between community and peace movements, also with marked woman leadership, which expresses itself in "nuclear free" communities for instance. Again, environmental/ecological/green movements in the West share compatible goals and membership with women's, peace, and community movements.

Therefore, these women's, peace, environmental, and community movements—all of which shy away from pursuit of state power and most entanglements with political institutions—offer widespread opportunities for coalitions among social movements. Moreover thanks to their preponderance of women, they also manifest more communal, participatory, democratic, mutual support, and networking instead of hierarchical relations among their participants and offer hope for their greater spread through society.

Other areas of overlap, shared membership, and compatibility or coalition may be observed among some religious and ethnic/national and sometimes racial movements. The movement led by the Ayatollah Khomeini in Iran and some of his followers elsewhere in the Islamic world is the most spectacular example, which has the most massive and successful mobilization of recent times to its credit. The sikhs in Punjab, the tamils in Sri Lanka, and perhaps Solidarity in Poland, Albanians in Yugoslav Kosovo, and Irish Catholics in Northern Ireland are other recent examples. Notably, however, these religious-ethnic-nationalist movements also seek state power or institutional autonomy and sometimes incorporation with a neighboring ethnic/national state. If communities are religiously and ethnically homogeneous, there may be overlap or coalition with these larger movements.

Opportunities for compatibility or coalition among different social movements are enhanced and may be found when they have common participants/membership and/or common enemies. The common membership of women in general in various different social movements has already been noted above. However, common membership also extends to individuals and particularly to individual women, who dedicate active participation to various social movements at the same time and/or successively. These people are in key positions to forge links if not coalitions among otherwise different social movements. Such links can also emerge from the identification of one or more common enemies, such as a particular state, government, or tyrant; a certain dominant institution or social, racial, or ethnic group; or even less concretely identifiable enemies such as "the West," "imperialism," "capital," "the state," "foreigners," "men," "authority," or "hierarchy." Moreover, both the opportunities for coalition and the massiveness and strength of social mobilization are probably enhanced when people perceive that they must defend themselves against these enemies.

There are also significant areas of conflict and competition among social movements. Of course, movements of different religions and ethnicities or races conflict and compete with each other. However, all of them also seem to conflict and compete with the women's movement(s) and often with the peace movement. In particular, virtually all religious, ethnic, and national(ist) movements—like working-class and Marxist oriented movements and political parties as well—negate and sacrifice women's interests. Moreover, they successfully compete with women's movements, which lose ground they may already have gained to the onslaught of religious, ethnic, and nationalist movements. Religion and nationalism, and even more so the two combined, seem to sacrifice women's interests and movements. Shi'ite Iran deliberately increases women's oppression. In Vietnam, Nicaragua, and elsewhere, women first participated actively in and benefited from nationalist struggle, but subsequently also saw further advances of their interests sacrificed to the priority of "the national interest" and in Nicaragua also to Catholic support. Similarly, nationalist and national liberation movements in many parts of Asia and Africa tend to overlook and neglect or even to suppress and combat minority ethnic and other movements and their interests.

Often, social movements also have serious internal conflicts of ends and/or means. Of course, when social movements are coalitions, especially for temporary tactical purposes, the participants may have different and sometimes conflicting ends and/or preferences among means. These have been common, for instance, among anti-imperialist national liberation and socialist movements in the third world. The combination of religious with other social movements, such as those with significant elements of liberation theology, also contain the potential for internal conflict. Indeed, most religious or strongly religiously oriented movements seem to contain important seeds of internal conflict between progressive and regressive, and sometimes also escapist, aims. Appeal to religion, not to mention a church, may be the main or even the only recourse for people to mobilize against a repressive regime or to overcome oppressive and/or alienating circumstances. In this sense, religion offers a liberating progressive option, like liberation theology and church-related community movements in Latin America, the Polish Catholic church, the movement against the Shah in Iran, and some ethnic/religious communal (defense) movements in Asia. However, the *same* religion and church also contains important regressive and reactionary elements. Regressive or even escapist elements are the offer to bring back to golden age of seventh-century Islam or even to eliminate all traces of Westernization. Literally reactionary are the Islamic and Catholic attempts to turn back or prevent the further development of progressive developments in gender relations, including divorce, birth control, and socioeconomic opportunities for women, and other civil rights and liberties. Indeed, religion is more often an instrument of reactionary than of progressive forces in the West, East, and South.

New Characteristics, Moral Motivation, and Social Power

Despite all these differences among contemporary social movements we can identify some ideal types and common characteristics. (We refer to "ideal" types in the Weberian sense of an analytic distillation of characteristics not found in their pure form in the real world.) We may distinguish movements that are offensive (a minority) and defensive (the majority). On a related but different dimension, we can identify progressive, regressive, and escapist movements. A third dimension or characteristic seems to be the preponderance of women rather than men—and therefore apparently less hierarchization in the movements, membership or leadership. A fourth dimension is that of armed struggle, especially for state power, or unarmed and especially nonviolent struggle, be it defensive or offensive. It can be no coincidence that the armed movements coincide with more hierarchical ones and the unarmed ones with movements in which women's participation is preponderant (even if women also participate in armed struggle).

A fifth dimension of special contemporary interest is the movements' national/transnational scope. Although many movements are local, even localist and nationalist, and seek to influence the action of particular states; much movement activity and scope is also transnational. By that we mean that movement concerns and communication are nether limited to the nation state, nor intentionally *inter*national, but that they are *non-* or *transnational* in escaping or transcending nation-state schema. Thus, particularly the women's, peace, and ecological movements, but also youth culture/movements increasingly have a transnational (and trans-ideological extrasystemic) global appeal and resonance far beyond the supposed "workers of the world unite" of old.

Other characteristics of movements are that few are at once offensive, in the sense of seeking to change the established order, and progressive in the sense of seeking a better order for themselves or the world. Most movements by far are defensive. Many seek to safeguard recent (sometimes progressive) achievements against reversal or encroachment. Examples are the student movements (which in 1986–87 reappeared in France, Spain, Mexico, and China in masses not seen since 1967–68) and many thousands of third world community movements seeking to defend their members' livelihood against the encroachment of economic crisis and political repression. Some defensive movements seek to defend the environment or to maintain peace, or both, like the Greens in Germany. Other movements react defensively against modern encroachments by offering to regress to an (often largely mythical) golden age, like seventh-century Islam. Many movements are escapist, or have important such components, in that they defensively/offensively seek millenarian salvation from the trials and tribulations of the real world, as in religious cults.

Varied as these social movements have been and are, if there are any characteristics they have in common, they are that they share the force of morality and a sense of (in)justice in individual motivation and the force of social mobilization in developing social power. Individual membership or participation and motivation in all sorts of social movements contains a strong moral component and defensive concern with justice in the social or world order. Social movements then mobilize their members in an offensive/defense against a shared moral sense of the injustice, as analyzed in Barrington Moore's *Injustice: The Social Bases of Obedience and Revolt.* Morality and jutice/injustice, perhaps more than the deprivation of livelihood and/or identity through exploitation and oppression through which morality and (in)justice manifest themselves, have probably been the essential motivating and driving force of social movements both past and present. However, this morality and concern with (in)justice refers largely to "us." The social group perceived as "we" was and is very variable as between the family, tribe, village, ethnic group, nation, country, first-second-or third world, humanity, and so forth, and gender, class, stratification, caste, race, and other groupings, or combinations of these. What mobilizes us is this deprivation/oppression/and especially injustice to "us," however "we" define and perceive ourselves. Each social movement then serves not only to combat deprivation but in so doing also to (re)affirm the identity of those active in the movement and perhaps also those "we" for whom the movement is active. Thus, such social movements, far from being new, have characterized human social life in many times and places.

A *new characteristic* of many contemporary social movements, however, is that—beyond that spontaneous appearing changeability and adaptability—they inherit organizational capacity and leadership from old labor movements, political parties, churches, and other organizations, from which they draw leadership cadres who became disillusioned with the limitations of the old forms and who now seek to build new ones. This organizational input into the new social movements may be an important asset for them, compared to their historical more amateurishly (dis)organized forerunners, but it may also contain the seeds of future institutionalization of some contemporary movements.

What else may be new in the "new" social movements is perhaps that they now tend to be more single class or stratum movements—middle class in the West and popular working class in the South—than many of them were through the centuries. However, by that criterion of newness, the "classical" old working-class movements are also new and some contemporary ethnic, national, and religious movements are old, as we will observe when we discuss the class composition of social movements below.

A third new characteristic is the much more massive participation of women in social movements now than before. Women's participation has increased both absolutely and relative to that of men. This is the case not only in the women's movement(s) itself/themselves, but also in the peace, environmental, and community movements. For that reason also many contemporary social movements now also express more feminine and feminist demands. This (in more than one sense) progressive feminization of social movements also contributes to making their organization less hierarchical—which need not mean less organized!

Whether new or old, the "new social movements" today are by far what most mobilizes most people in pursuit of common concerns. Far more than "classical" class movements, the social movements motivate and mobilize hundreds of millions of people in all parts of the world—mostly outside established political and social institutions that people find inadequate to serve their needs—which is why they have recourse to "new" largely non-institutionalized social movements. This popular movement to social movements is manifest even in identity seeking and/or responsive social mobilization or social movement with little or no membership ties: in youth (movement?) response to rock music around the world and football in Europe and elsewhere; in the millions of people in country after country who have spontaneously responded to visits by the Pope (beyond the Catholic church as an institution); and in the massive spontaneous response to Bob Geldorf's extra (political) institutional Band Aid, Live Aid, and Sport Aid appeals against hunger in Africa. The latter was an appeal and response not only to compassion, but also to a moral sense of the (in)justice of it all.

However, not all people in movement necessarily constitute a social movement. Not every spontaneous mass meeting, crowd or riot—even when it expresses important social demands—is necessarily (the expression of) a social movement. Some such uprisings, as in 1988 in Burma, Armenia, Azerbijan, Yugoslavia, Algeria, may however offer the popular basis of a social movement in formation. Thus, some of these nonmembership forms of social mobilization have more in common with social movements than do some self-styled "movements." The Movimiento(s) de Izquierda Revolucionaria (MIR) in Bolivia, Chile, Peru, and Venezuela, are (or were) really "Leninist" democratic *centralist* political parties. The Sandinista "movement" in Nicaragua formed a coalition of mass organizations. All sought to capture and manage state power. The nonaligned movement is a coalition of states or their governments in power and certainly not a *social* movement or a liberation *movement* of the peoples themselves.

Significantly, social movements generate and wield social power through their social mobilization of their participants. This social power is at once generated by and derived from the social *movement* itself, rather than from any institution, political or otherwise. Indeed, institutionalization weakens social movements and state political power negates them (although institutional and political allies outside the movements can help protect them or support their goals with the powers that be). Social movements require flexible, adaptive, and autonomous nonauthoritarian organization to direct social power in pursuit of social goals, which cannot be pursued only through random spontaneity. Such flexible organization, however, need not imply institutionalization, which confines and constricts the social movements' social power. Thus, the autonomous, self-organizing, new social movements confront existing (state) political power through new social power, which modifies political power. The recognition of the women's movement that the personal is political applies a forteriori to *social* movements, which also redefine political power. Thus, even though not all that moves is necessarily a movement, Luciana Castellina, a participant in many social movements (and some political parties) correctly observed that "we are a movement because we move"— even political power.

Civil Democracy and Social Transformation

Thus, multiple kinds of social LEF/S movements emerge and mobilize to rewrite the institutional (democratic?) political power rules of the game. Indeed, thereby they redefine the game itself and increasingly rely on and incorporate new democratic social/civil power rules of the game in civil society. In so doing, they also help to shift the sociopolitical center of gravity from institutional political or economic democracy (or other power) in the state toward more participatory civil democracy and power in civil society and culture. This participatory civil democracy is importantly carried by women, but it extends far beyond the family and home to other concerns where women also have a relatively greater presence and more important role than in the polity and economy.

There are enormous and perhaps growing areas of civil LEF/S concerns where political citizen reliance on institutional political state power and its capture through political revolution is inadequate or downright counterproductive. In these areas, the civil/social and ever more female citizens of civil society increasingly democratically pursue their varied and often conflicting economic, social, gender, community, cultural, ethnic, religious, ideological, and other sometimes also political LEF/S concerns. To these ends, the citizens of civil society form and mobilize themselves through equally varied autonomous and self-empowering *social* movements and *non-party* or *non-governmental* organizatins. Alternatively these movements and organizations rely on self empowerment seeking to modify state action, as in South Korea, Burma, Chile, USSR, and elsewhere in 1988.

Everywhere in the world today, West, East, and South, *democracy* has become the principal and most universal political rallying cry. Democracy may be said to replace most LEF/S demands today and increasingly to displace other demands like "liberty," "socialism," and "development." Perhaps democracy does not yet replace rallies to nationalist and ethnic identities, but today even these also appeal often to democracy to further their particular(ist) ends. At the same time and partly as a result however, to promote democracy people everywhere also rely increasingly on their own and others self-empowering active democratic participation in civil society. In so doing they also demand the extension of democracy to civil society or the redefinition of democracy to include civil democracy. (We hesitate to call these demands for "social" democracy because this term has already been preempted—and misused?—in another political (party) sense).

In the West, the increase in participatory civil democracy is also accompanied by or reflected in declining voter participation in party political elections. In the East, new democracy is manifested in civil social movements in China and tens of thousands of new civil "clubs" and "non-official" organizations as well as massive public demonstrations under glasnost beyond the party in the Soviet Union and Eastern Europe. (Indeed, much of Gorbachev's perestroika and glasnost are promoted outside of and even against the Communist Party of the Soviet Union). In the South, individual and massive participation in movements and organizations to reshape civil society and culture are taking pride of place next to the capture and management of state power, where democracy is increasingly missed.

Thus, in this democratic *process* the importance of autonomous participatory civil democracy in (often sub- but also transnational) civil society also increases relative to political party democracy in the nation-state. Therefore, self-empowering participatory social movements (with growing women's participation) also participate increasingly in this process of social transformation.

This also means that social movements are likely (even destined?) to play increasingly important roles in future social transformation to the extent that it is the result not only of environmental, technological and other transformatory forces largely beyond direct social control, but also of voluntary/ist social action and intervention. For lack of adequate institutional(ized) means therefore, social movements increasingly become the vehicle of present and future direct social intervention and participatory democracy. They also replace or supersede some other institutional forms of social expression and action, at least temporarily, especially during times of acute social crisis or rapid social transition. Finally, social movements also intervene to transform existing, or form new, social institutions themselves.

Thus social movements, even more than political parties or state formation/management, now appear increasingly as the vehicles and forms of voluntary transformatory advance toward "socialism," if any. Perhaps ironically, moreover, the very life-cycle of social movements, which either fade away or become institutionalized, is less a mark of their weakness, irrelevance, or self-negation, than it is the living expression of their vitality for and growing importance in the social transformation(s) of the future.

References Cited

Brand, Karl-Werner. 1988. "Cyclical Aspects of New Social Movements. Modernization-Critical Moods and Mobilization Cycles of New Middle-Class Radicalism." In Russell Dalton and Manfred Kuchler, eds, *Challenging the Political Order.*
―――. 1987. "Historical Antecedents of New Social Movements in Britain, Germany, and the United States." Paper prepared for a seminar on New Social Movements in Talahassee, Florida, April 2–4, 1987, available from the author at Institut für Sozialwissenschaften, Technische Universität Mänchen, Lothstr. 17, 8000 München 2, Germany.
Eisler, Riane. 1987. *The Chalice and the Blade.* San Francisco: Harper & Row.
Frank, Andre Gunder. 1972. *Lumpenbourgeoisie: Lumpendevelopment.* New York: Monthly Review Press.
―――. 1967. *Capitalism and Underdevelopment in Latin America.* New York: Monthly Review Press.
Frank, Andre Gunder and Marta Fuentes. 1987. "Nine Theses on Social Movements." *IFDA Dossier* (Lyon/Geneva) 63 (January 1987).
Friberg, Mats. 1987. "Four Waves of Political Mobilization in Europe." Paper presented at UNU Workshop on Social Movements in Gothenburg, Sweden, available from the author at Department of Peace and Conflict Research, University of Gothenburg, Sweden.
Fuentes, Marta and Andre Gunder Frank. 1989. "Ten Theses on Social Movements." *World Development* Washington/Oxford, February 1989.
Gattei, Giorgio, 1989. "Every 25 Years? Strike Waves and Long Economic Cy-

cles." Paper presented at the International colloquium on "The Long Waves of the Economic Conjuncture—The Present State of the Debate," Brussels, January 12–24, Series 2.

Goldstein, Joshua S. 1987. *Long Cycles. Prosperity and War in the Modern Age.* New Haven and London: Yale University Press.

Goldstone, Jack A. 1980. "The Weakness of Organization: A New Look at Gamson's *The Strategy of Social Protest.*" *American Journal of Sociology* 85 (March).

Huber, Joseph. 1987. "Soziale Bewegungen," paper available from author at Mommsenstr. 2, 1000 Berlin 12, Germany.

Huizer, Gerrit. 1980. *Peasant Movements and their Counterforces in South-East Asia.* New Delhi: Marwah Publications.

———. 1972. *The Revolutionary Potential of Peasants in Latin America.* Lexington, MA: Lexington Books.

Langer, William L. 1952. *An Encyclopedia of World History.* Boston: Houghton Mifflin. New ed. 1972.

Li Guoguang. 1988. "Developing Marxist Theory in the Practice of Reform." *Social Sciences in China* 1 (March).

Ma Ji. 1988. "The Primary Stage of Socialism and the Development of Marxism-A Summary of a Discussion by Theoreticians, Journalists and Publishers in Beijing." *Social Sciences in China* 1 (March).

Moore Jr., Barrington. 1978. *Injustice. The Social Bases of Obedience and Revolt.* White Plains, NY: M.E. Sharpe.

Mukherjee, Mridula, 1988. "Peasant Resistance and Peasant Consciousness in Colonial India." *Economic and Political Weekly* (Bombay), October 8.

van Roon, Rob. 1988. "Lange Golven in Sociale Conflicten?" ISMOG-University of Amsterdam research paper.

Rowbotham, Sheila. 1973. *Hidden From History: 300 Years of Women's Oppression and the Fight Against It.* London: Pluto Press.

Schram, Stuart, 1988. "Political Reform in China—In the Primary Stage of Socialism." *IHJ Bulletin* 8, no. 2 (Spring).

Silver, Beverly. 1989. "Class Struggle and the Kondratieff." Paper presented at the International colloquium on "The Long Waves of the Economic Conjuncture—The Present State of the Debate," Brussels, January 12–24.

Taylor, Barbara. 1983. *Eve and the New Jerusalem. Socialism and Feminism in the Nineteenth Century.* London: Virago Press.

Tarrow, Sidney. 1983. *Struggling to Reform: Social Movements and Policy Change During Cycles of Protest.* Cornell Center for International Studies Occasional Paper No. 15.

Wolf, Eric. 1968. *Peasant Wars of the Twentieth Century.* New York: Harper & Row.

Yu Guangyuan. 1988. "The Economy of the Primary Stage of Socialism." *Social Sciences in China* 2 (June).

CONCLUSION: A FRIENDLY DEBATE

Samir Amin, Giovanni Arrighi,
Andre Gunder Frank, and Immanuel Wallerstein

The very wide agreement in basic approach among the authors is accompanied by some significant divergences, which cannot have escaped the reader. We think it useful nonetheless to spell out four of them. These divergences are never total, but they do reflect important differences of emphasis.

The first of these divergences concerns our respective perceptions of the historical development of capitalism as a world-system, from which derive differences in perception of the role that the movements—antisystemic, social, popular—have played in this historical development.

For Amin, Arrighi, and Wallerstein, the creation of a capitalist world-economy in the sixteenth century, located originally in Europe but expanding subsequently to cover the globe, represented a major historical rupture, involving the establishment of an historical system that was qualitatively different from the many historical systems that had hitherto existed.

The capitalist system of course had patterns which could be analyzed. It was however also in a process of constant development and transformation. It thus contained within itself, as do all historical systems, certain basic contradictions. This meant that, eventually, the system would find itself unable to contain these contradictions by further adjustments, would therefore be in "crisis," and would somehow come to an end, to be succeeded by one or multiple other historical systems.

Given this kind of a model of historical development, the role of the movements within the capitalist world-economy seems quite straightforward. They were themselves products of the system, one way of its adjusting to its contradictions. They represented primarily a political force for change, becoming strong in the late nineteenth century and even stronger in the twentieth. These movements were often successful, in the sense that, as a result of the political struggles, structural changes occurred in all the arenas of social life—in the construction of the markets, in the social relations at the workplaces, in the political organization of the states, and in the multiple cultural arenas.

182 Conclusion

These structural changes, whether they be labeled reforms or revolutions, mattered. They brought about some positive improvements in the life patterns of the world's working classes, and this was primarily to the credit of the movements who fought for these structural changes. Obviously, the structural changes had their limits, their ambiguities, even their negative sides. Obviously, too, it is not necessarily the case today that the strategies adopted in the nineteenth century would be fruitful if continued today. We can hold that view, however, without necessarily feeling that the nineteenth-century strategies were inappropriate at the time.

Finally, in part because of the activities of the movements, in part because of other developments, according to Amin, Arrighi, and Wallerstein, the breakdown or "demise" of the capitalist world-economy is most probable during the twenty-first century. They believe that the major uncertainty is not whether or not there will be a demise, but what is in store for us as the succession.

While Frank does not dissent entirely from this historical sketch—indeed he shares much of it—he thinks it is quite overdrawn in its sharpness; and this at all three points in time—at the onset of, during the life of, and at the prospective end of this historical system.

Frank now thinks, having revised his earlier views about the world-system, that the creation of a capitalist world-economy marked less of a qualitative historical rupture than is usually argued, and, moreover, that whatever change it represented started earlier than the sixteenth century. Frank now thinks that there has existed a very large single world-historical system, at least in Afro-Eurasia, for several thousand years. He argues that while important changes occurred in the sixteenth century that led to the worsening of conditions in what is now called the third world, these changes were less a qualitative systemic transformation starting in Europe than a shift of the system's core from East to West.

It follows from this view of the sixteenth-century happenings that Frank (and Fueutes) also take a less dramatic view of the impact of the movements in the nineteenth and twentieth centuries. Yes, the movements struggled, and yes, they won some victories. But Frank tends to think that these victories were mostly tactical rather than fundamental, and that they accomplished less structural change than their members themselves (or Amin, Arrighi, and Wallerstein) think. Frank expresses reservations at what he takes to be Arrighi's contention that, at some points in history, the movements have gained an upper hand over world economic forces. He regards the latter as always operative and determinant, albeit in different ways at different times.

Finally, looking forward to the twenty-first century, Frank tends to feel that Amin, Arrighi, and Wallerstein are too rosy in their predictions. He is not sure that the dominant forces of the capitalist world-economy will have exhausted their ingenuity and therefore their ability to keep the system operating. And while not being a total Cassandra, he is even less optimistic than the others about the likelihood that the eventual successor system or systems will turn out to be more progressive.

The second major divergence concerns the historic importance of the struggle by the movements for state power, and for some form of delinking from the system. Here, however, the line-up is somewhat different. It is Arrighi, Frank, and Wallerstein who tend to share the same (or similar) views, and Amin who takes a somewhat different position.

All the authors agree that the bulk of the movements—especially those whose goals were either proletarian power or national liberation—did tend to pursue coming to state power in one way or another. And all of them agree that, in fact, very many of these movements did in fact come to state power (although in Frank's arithmetic there are fewer such cases than in the arithmetic of the other three).

There are, however, two questions: "How much good did achieving state power do? and, Does it remain a plausible and desirable strategy today? For Arrighi, Frank, and Wallerstein, the benefits that have been derived from obtaining state power are questionable. Amin, on the other hand, tends to take a globally positive view of this coming to state power.

We must, however, nuance this picture. Amin agrees that there have been many negative aspects of past experiences—insufficient delinking from the world-system, grievous abuses and absence of internal democracy, intellectual rigidities and dogmatism. Yet, when all is said and done, he says, there were real achievements. The USSR and China did delink, he argues, and even if they didn't create socialism, they are better off for having delinked (as is everyone else for the fact of their having delinked). Whatever the ups and downs of the policies pursued by their governments, their societies will probably impose on the governments the submission of their external relations (even if intensified) to the logic of their specific internal choices. In that sense, they are not prepared to reintegrate into the world-system and return to capitalism. In that sense, 1917 did not inaugurate a mere bracket in history which is now ending, but launched the era of postcapitalism.

184 Conclusion

The other three disagree, but to varying extents. Frank is the most opposite in his appreciations. He casts a jaundiced eye on almost all the experiences in which movements have assumed state power, and does not believe that either the USSR or China have ever really delinked; he doubts indeed whether it is possible at all for single states, even the largest and strongest, to delink.

Wallerstein and Arrighi are somewhere in-between, but probably closer to Frank than to Amin. They take a less uniformly jaundiced view of all experiences of assumption of state power, but they are far from sanguine about the merits of most of these experiences. Let us say that they see some limited good as having occurred as a result of these experiences, but often a great deal of harm as well. In any case they surely do not feel that the achievement of state power should, in the future, continue to be a centerpiece of movement strategy.

On the issue of historic delinking, Wallerstein tends to be in substantial agreement with Frank about the USSR, China, and other similar cases. They never really delinked, and to the extent that they seemed to have delinked, it was largely forced upon them. Economic processes continued to be subject to the law of value. Arrighi would not put it that way. He believes that one might say that, up to a point, the USSR and China did delink, but it was temporary. He thinks it extremely doubtful that delinking is a viable strategy for the future.

The third divergence of the four authors concerns the periodization of the history of the movements. Once again, the lines of divergence shift. Arrighi, in his essay, has spelled out three major periods in the history of the movements: 1848–96, 1896–1948, and post-1948. Each of these periods differs considerably from the others in its political and economic realities. Consequently, the strategies of the movements have been different during each of these periods, which happen to coincide more or less with full Kondratieff cycles, an A-period plus a B-period. Amin is substantially in agreement with the periodization.

Wallerstein, however, sees only two periods, one going from 1848 to 1968, and a second beginning in 1968. These dates are based on the assumption that 1848 and 1968 mark two *world-systemic* revolutionary upsurges, and that each resulted in a major debate among the movements as to appropriate strategy in the light of the lessons of those world-events. In the first case, the debate was resolved by a large consensus. A particular strategy, that of pursuing state power, became dominant. In the second case, the debate is still going on. It is therefore unsure what consensus will result, if any.

Frank sees really only one period, perhaps starting earlier than 1848. He see no subsequent dividing points, no significant shifts in movement policy, but rather the ups and downs of the movements, as documented in the chapter he and Fuentes have written. Frank's position derives quite clearly from his position on the historical development of the capitalist world-economy as a whole. Since, as we have seen, he is somewhat skeptical about the overall achievements of the movements heretofore, he finds little utility in the periodizations of the others, which presume a greater degree of movement accomplishment.

The fourth important divergence among us concerns the picture we draw of future developments of the movements. We observed in the introduction that the division of labor among us was not simply a formula for technical efficacity, but reflected the differences in our emphases. There is actually a four-way divergence about the future. Let us put it crudely first, and then try to soften the edges. For Arrighi, the future lies with workers' movements; for Amin, with national popular movements; for Frank, with the "other" movements which he and Fuentes think are the only ones that deserve the name of "social movements"; and for Wallerstein, in a self-conscious federation of all three kinds of movements.

This is, however, too crude a formulation. All of us believe there has been and will be a certain complementarity in the role of different kinds of movements. And none of us wish to be associated with some of the sectarian definitions that have often been proferred concerning what does or does not constitute a workers' movement or a national popular movement or a social movement (in the usage of the term specified by Frank and Fuentes). Nonetheless, the image of the near future that each presents is somewhat different.

Arrighi, for reasons spelled out in his essay, argues that the geographical disjuncture of the loci of immiseration and the loci of workers' social power is decreasing. As a consequence, the working classes throughout the world are coming to face similar situations, and therefore their movements will all begin to center their demands around the capital-labor conflict. In this sense, they will all be workers' movements. But, Arrighi insists, they will not at all look like "classical" workers' movements, since the bulk of the world's salaried working classes will now be composed of women, "minorities," and the like. Thus, the women's movement and the movements of "minorities" will be a workers' movement because the workers' movement will be a movement composed primarily of women and "minorities."

Amin's anticipations are not quite the same. He believe that continuing polarization of capitalism will continue to take a spatial form. Therefore, he believes movements in the core and movements in the periphery will continue to be different from each other in important ways. As a result, he maintains his view that the revolutionary dynamic remains primarily in the periphery and that the major strategy will continue to be delinking. Nonetheless, he emphasizes that delinking will take forms in the future that may be quite different from earlier attempts at autarky. He suspects that the major device will be to develop non-linked endogenous technology. While recognizing that movements in the core countries may sometimes play a progressive role, he considers that, even when this is so, they will remain a secondary factor in the world-transformation process. Therefore the true challenge which the progressive movements are facing can be formulated as follows: Will they accept the further global centralization of wealth and power through the market mechanism, or will they gradually impose a polycentric world?

Frank starts with the greatest suspicion of all state-oriented tactics. This is why he is willing to call "social movements" only those movements which put forward a strategy that does *not* involve taking state power (or at least those for whom it is not a primary goal). He is hopeful about the future, because he sees this kind of "social movement" growing in strength and support throughout the world. They may flourish because they will *not* be primarily workers' movements (even in Arrighi's revised sense) or national liberation movements.

Finally, Wallerstein started with a different morphology and thereupon comes to a different conclusion. He sees three "old" varieties of movements that flourished from 1848 to 1968. Each came to power, more or less, in one of the three political "worlds," largely after 1945: Social-Democrats in the West, Communists in the East, national liberation movements in the South. For Wallerstein, all three shared the same basic strategy of obtaining state power as the intermediate step. All three were challenged in the post-1968 period by three "new" kinds of movements: the so-called new social movements in the West; the "antibureaucratic" movements in the East; and the "anti-Enlightenment" movements in the South. All the "new" movements specifically questioned the basic strategic option of the "old" movements. He sees all six varieties engaged currently in a gigantic debate about future strategy. The optimal result would be to operationalize the concept of a "family of movements" that would work in some kind of relative unison.

Still and all, each of us, when presented with each other's visions of the immediate future, is ready to admit some truth in the other vision, some uncertainty about our own, and some sense that history once again may reserve its surprises.

We close this book once again on the same profession of faith we made in the previous one. A better world-system is possible (not certain, but possible). This world-system will be better to the degree that it is more democratic and more egalitarian. We accept as our own the motto of the movements in Portuguese-speaking Africa: A luta continua.